JOURNAL OF SAMUEL MACLAY

METALMARK BOOKS

JOURNAL

OF

SAMUEL MACLAY,

WHILE SURVEYING

THE WEST BRANCH OF THE SUSQUEHANNA, THE SINNEMAHONING AND THE ALLEGHENY RIVERS,

In 1790.

———

PUBLISHED BY

JOHN F. MEGINNESS.

———

WILLIAMSPORT, PA.:

GAZETTE AND BULLETIN PRINTING HOUSE.

1887.

TO THE READER.

The journal of Hon. Samuel Maclay, printed in full for the first time after a lapse of 97 years, will be found both interesting and valuable. After his death, in Buffalo Valley, in 1811, the journal passed into the hands of his son, Hon. William P. Maclay, who settled in Mifflin County, and died there in 1884, at a ripe age. The journal finally became the property of Hon. David Maclay, of Sligo, Clarion County, a grandson. He, like his distinguished grandfather, served in the State Senate. In 1872–3–4–5 he represented the XXVIIth Senatorial District in the Legislature. He is now about 68 years of age.

The journal is written in a small, distinct, business hand, with some peculiarities. The final "e's" are written with an "i," and where double "l's" are used the last letter is only half the size of the first. The book looks as if it was a home-made production. It is of unruled, unsized paper, and consists of two parts tied together, and unequal in size. Its dimensions are about 3 by 5 inches. As a relic of the illustrious Maclay family, whose early history is so interwoven with that of the West Branch Valley, it cannot fail to be highly prized by the descendants, and to be read with deep interest by all lovers of local history.

In laying it before the public, the publisher desires to acknowledge his indebtedness to George J. Reid, Esq., of Clarion, for valuable assistance.

THE PUBLISHER.

SINNEMAHONING CANOE.

JOURNAL OF HON. SAMUEL MACLAY.

While Surveying the West Branch of the Susquehanna, the Sinnemahoning and Allegheny Rivers.

ANNOTATED BY JOHN F. MEGINNESS.

[On April 9, 1790, Samuel Maclay, Timothy Matlack and John Adlum were commissioned by the Supreme Executive Council of Pennsylvania to examine the head waters of the Susquehanna, explore the streams of the New Purchase, i. e. the Northwestern section of the State lately purchased from the Indians, and to discover if possible a route for a road to connect the waters of the Allegheny with the West Branch of the Susquehanna. Samuel Maclay was born June 17, 1741, in Lurgan Township, Franklin County. Little is known of his early life. In 1767-8 he was employed as a deputy surveyor for his brother, Hon. William Maclay. In 1769 he appears as an assistant to his brother on the surveys of the officer's tract in Buffalo Valley. He surveyed largely in what is now Mifflin County, and took up a good deal of land there. Mr. Maclay was Lieutenant Colonel of a Battalion of Associators, and as such was a delegate, with McLanachan, Geddes and Brady, to the convention at Lancaster, July 4, 1776, which elected two brigadiers and organized the Associators, the then militia of the State. In 1792 he was appointed one of the associate judges of Northumberland County, and resigned December 17, 1795. In October, 1794, he was a candidate for Congress and carried the county by 1,100 majority. The vote was only 2,850. In Buffalo he had 464, to 14 for his opponent, John Andre Hanna. He served for the years 1795-6. On the 2d of December, 1801, Mr. Maclay was elected Speaker of the Senate, and re-elected December 7, 1802. On the 14th he was elected United States Senator, and, being Speaker, had to sign his own certificate. In January, 1803, he presided at the impeachment trial of Judge Addison, and continued acting as Speaker—against the protest of the opposition, however, after March—until March 16th, when he resigned that position, and on the 2d of September his position as State Senator. He resigned his seat in the United States Senate on the 4th of January, 1809. Mr. Maclay was very popular in his manners, a good scholar and writer. He had an extensive library containing many valuable books. He was always of the people and for the people, plain and simple in his manner, disliking ostentation. It is related of him that on one occasion he brought a handsome coach home from Lancaster, and the family took it to Buffalo Church next Sabbath. He noticed the impression it made on the people, and that coach never left the carriage house again. It rotted down where it was put away that

Sunday evening. He was a large man, resembling Henry Clay very much, though much stouter in later years. Mr. Maclay's wife was Elizabeth Plunkett, born in 1755, whose lineage is traceable to John Harris, senior. Mrs. Maclay died in 1823. Mr. Maclay died at his residence in Buffalo Valley October 5, 1811, aged 70 years, 3 months and 18 days, and was buried on his farm. The brick wall enclosing the grave is within sight from the turnpike, after passing the New Berlin road, a short distance West of Lewisburg. A handsome monument marks his last resting place.—*Linn's Annals of Buffalo Valley*, pp. 401–2–3–4.

Mr. Maclay's diary begins with his departure from Buffalo Valley down the Susquehanna. After reaching the Swatara, he was to ascend that stream to Lebanon and there meet the other commissioners.]

Memoran'm, April, 1790.—The* 20th, 21st, 22d, 23d, 24th spent in providing for the Expedition, enquiring for hands, Boat, &c.

On the 26th.—Started with James McLaughlin's Boat; he and Edward Sweney and Matthew Gray taken into pay.

TUESDAY 27th.—Expences at Herold's for four Breakfasts and one quart whiskey £0, 5s, 2d.

HARRISBURG, April 27th.—Cash paid for one-half pint Gin (£)0, 1s, 0d.

MIDDLETOWN, April 27th.—At night. Supper, Lodgings and Breakfast for three men, paid Wolfley 9s, 11d.

The 28th.—Attempted to go up the Suatara with the Boat. Got the Boat over Mr. Fry's Mill Dam; the day grew so stormey that I was obliged to return to Middletown. Bought a Gammon of Bacon from Mr. Fry but were unable to Eat it; the hog must have had the measels. Paid at Fry's and Wolfley's 4s.

APRIL 29th.—Set off from Middletown early in the morning; found the Suatara in Good Boatable order, and in General Good Boatable water from George Fry's Dam. The only inconvenience is the Bottom, Rocky and smooth; the men often missed their set.

---

* Mr. Maclay paid little regard to punctuation and was careless in spelling. The first word in many of his sentences begins with a small letter. For the sake of appearance and connection this defect and that of punctuation have been remedied in copying. Otherwise the text strictly follows the original in orthography.

We stopped at a house about three o'clock and got a hasty Dinner of Bacon & Egs for which I paid 2s, 6d.

We reached the mouth of the Quitapahela* a little Before sunset; took our Boat about a fourth of a mile up it and stoped for the night.

APRIL 30th.—Took an early Breakfast for which I paid 3s, 9d. Left our boat and Baggage, Started on foot, took nearly an East corse, came to the Quitapahela in about one mile; its corse then Nearly N. W. It appeared to be sufficient in depth to carry a Boat of about 5 ton Burden; the current appeared to be Brisk in general all the way up to John Myer's mill dam. This dam is Raised about 6 feet and dams the water up as high as the foording at the west end of Millerstown which foording is about 20 perches Below the dam of Old's Ironworks; there we took the Road. There is another Mill dam opposite Millers town which Belongs to Abraham Regile. Nine o'clock. Stoped at the Sign of the Boar in Millers Town at James Long's. Drank 2 quarts of Syder for which I paid 1s, 9d. Started again and came to Lebanon at one o'clock. Got dinner but heard nothing from the commissioner (s).

MAY 1st.—Waited until after Dinner, then walked Down the Reading Road but could neither hear from or see the commissioners. Returned, waited, and kept looking out but to no effect. About sunset Capt'n Moore arrived from Philadelphia. Sent the Landlord Grenawalt to inquire at Capt'n Moore; he returned and informed me that Capt'n Moore had seen Col'n Matlack† in Phila-

---

*The Quitapahilla is a branch of the Big Swatara in Lebanon County. According to Heckewelder it is corrupted from *Cuitpehella,* or *Cuwitpehella,* signifying, in the Delaware Indian dialect, a spring that flows from the ground among pines.

†Timothy Matlack was born of Quaker parentage at Haddonfield, New Jersey, in 1730. At an early period he settled in Philadelphia. After the Revolution we find him a prominent member of the Society of Free Quakers, and chiefly instrumental in building the meeting house, southwest corner of Fifth and Arch Streets, in that city. He was a member of the Provincial Conference held at Carpenters' Hall, June 18, 1775; and of the Convention of July 15, 1776. Under the Constitution framed by the latter body, he was appointed Secretary of the

delphia, that Col. Matlack had Either told him he would start from
Philadelphia on Thursday next or that he intended to be at this
place on that day but was uncertain which, & told him that the
weather had been so unfavorable that he Expected the other commissioner would not attend agreeable to the appointment. This
Intelligence with the circumstances attending it Embrasses me
much. Here I am with three hands at Expenses, 12 miles from
our Boat, without any Instrument proper for the Business I came
on; among a number of People not overly Polite to strangers, near
one Hundred miles from home; to return home, shameful; to stay
disagreeable and altogether uncertain. Not a single line from my
Coleagues either to apologize, or to assign a reason why they did
not attend or to appoint another day.

SUNDAY, May 2d.—Breakfasted at Grenewalts and then walked
back as far as the Sign of the Bear at Millers Town. Drank some
cyder; felt Fatigued. Sent James Sweney and Matthew Gray on
to the Boat and concluded to stay with Long's for the day, and
kept McLaughlin with me as he complained much of the Rheumatick pains in his knees. Went to Bed, Slept 2 hours, Got up but
felt no appetite for Dinner. Longed about until 5 o'clock; spoke
for a Dish of Coffee; with the Coffee the landlady brought a Dish

---

State, which office he held most of the time until March 25, 1783. In 1776 he
was in command of one of the Philadelphia Battalions of Associators, and in
active service. He was a member of the Council of Safety from July 24, 1776,
to March 13, 1777; and secretary of the same during the close of the latter year.
At the end of the Revolution Colonel Matlack was presented with a silver urn,
by the "Committee of Safety of the City," for his patriotic devotion to the cause
of freedom. He was one of the commissioners appointed to form the Flying
Camp, and in 1785, was directed to carry on the prosecution against the traitor
Arnold; was a member of the Old Congress of 1780–1, and on the 14th of April,
1800, appointed Master of the Rolls, an office he held until its abolishment by the
act of Assembly, March 29, 1809. He subsequently received the appointment of
prothonotary of one of the courts of the city of Philadelphia. Colonel Matlack
died near Holmesburg, on the 15th of April, 1829, at the very advanced age of
ninety-nine years; and his remains are interred in the Free Quaker burial
ground, on Fifth Street, north of Spruce, Philadelphia.—*Sketches of members of
the Constitutional Convention, in Pennsylvania Magazine of History, by Dr. Egle.*

of Bacon and Egs. The sight of this gave Edge to my appetite.
After Coffee smoked a pipe; was much diverted with the observa-
tions made by James McLaughlin on various subjects, in particular
on the Germany manners.

Paid at Lebanon for self and the 3 hands £1, 4s, 0d.

Paid at Millers Town for self and James McLaughlin, supper &
Breakfast 5s, 0d.

MONDAY, May 3d.—Set out after Breakfast from Millers Town;
walked about three milles. Stopped at a House near the Quitapahela Branch. Got a Drink of water. Rested about an hour
then walked on and came to our Boat at 12 o'clock; found the
Boys, Edw. Sweney and Mathew Gray. Got our Dinner, then
Proposed walking to Mr. McKnights; was informed that he lived
about two miles from our Boat; but the Evening began to be
stormy and threatened rain which determined me to continue for
the Night where I was.

TUESDAY, May 4th.—The morning Cloudy and cold but no Great
appearance of Rain. Felt more at a loss what to do than I ever
did. The hands all impatient and on the freet. McLaughlin said
he was as bad as if confined in Jail. Had not a book of any kind,
my almanack excepted, which I read more than onest over in order
to drive the time. The people where we were discovered a disposition to oblige but were ill Provided to accomodate Strangers.
About 10 o'clock it began to rain which made it still more disagreeable as I was then deprived of the Exercise of walking and
felt Indisposed with a headache. Day continued cloudy but rained
little; a kind of Disagreeable, raw, cold weather. About 3 o'clock
my headache Got worse; our landlady Brought me a Vial with
Camphoir with which I rubbed my Temples and found Immediate
Relief; Drank a dish of Coffee after which I felt Pretty well.

WEDNESDAY, May 5th.—The morning cloudy and no word from
the Commissioners; the afternoon cleared. Spent it Looking at

Edw. making and setting traps for the musk rats of which there appeared to be plenty in the Creek.

THURSDAY, May 6th.—The weather Still continued cloudy, though there was but little rain. Spent the morning in Preparing our landlords corn for planting with Tar; after it was tared I found that the fouls would not eat it and found that a small Quantity of Tar is sufficient, 3 Quarts I think plenty for a Bushel, and by dusting it with ashes after the Tar is put on it, it may be handled without any inconvenience from the Tar. Had some hopes that the commissioners had arrived at Lebanon yesterday; kept a look out for an Express but to no Effect. Afternoon rain began and continued until night; went to bed Extremely Fatigued with waiting.

FRIDAY, May 7th.—Rose early; felt Extremely Fatigued; head much out of order, Sholders and Legs sore and altogether unwell. Got our Breakfast, then walked about three Quarters of a mile up the Creek. Borrowed a Razor, Shaved my self and returned; a kind of Dizzyness still continued in my head & the aching in my Bones; althow in opinion I felt some Better. Yet no word from the commissioners; the mens patience Quite Exausted for want of something to do. I have now a full proof that having nothing to do is the most disagreeable Situation in this life; the mind for want of something to keep its powers Exerted, turns on itself and Destroys everything that has even the appearance of Injoyment.

After dinner set off with James McLaughlin and walked as far as Millerstown, to try what Exercise would do; after I stopped at Millers Town found the pain in my Bones, particularly in my shoulders increased and found myself altogether unsound. Was obliged to go to bed. Slept almost all night but in the morning Still felt that soreness continue.

SATURDAY, May 8th.—No account yet from the Commissioners. Still Quite unwell. Shoulders, Back and Right Side as sore as if

Brused; walked to the Quitaphela at Regiles' dam in order to deceive the time that was Exceedingly heavy. Rode out of town in a chase with my landlord; felt something better after my Return; about 8 o'clock at night heard by a Capt. Crain that the commissioners were arrived at Lebanon.

Expences at Millers town for self and James McLaughlin, £0, 1s, 9d.

Cash Lent Col. Matlack at Christopher Long's, 2s, 4d.

Cash paid at Crab's in Harrisburg, 2s, 4d.

* * * * * * *

(No entries for a week.)

MONDAY, May 17th.—This morning we set off early with our Boat. Passed Erwin's Boats at Herrold's Landing but were Immediately pursued by one of Erwin's Boats with Seven of their Boat hands on Board. The Chase continued for one hour at least; they did not exert themselves to such a degree as Toatally to Exaust themselves but Regulated their Exertions Just as they were necessary to keep ahead of the other boat. We arrived opposite Sunbury about 12 o'clock. Mr. Adlum* Left the Boat and Crossed to Sunbury but informed Colonel Matlack and myself that he

---

*Very little is known of the history of John Adlum. He was born in the town of York, Pa. His father was one of the earliest settlers at that place, and served as sheriff as early as 1749, and later as coroner of the county. He was a man of some prominence. Was one of the trustees for the erection of St John's Episcopal Church, and died shortly after its dedication, on the 30th of November, 1773, in his 74th year. The son (John Adlum) learned surveying, and in 1789 he was directed by Surveyor General Lukens to survey the reserved tracts of land at Presqu' Isle (Erie), Le Bœuf, &c. The same year he was appointed by the Government, on the recommendation of William Maclay, Benjamin Rush, John Nicholson and Colonel Thomas Hartley, a commissioner for examining the navigation of the Susquehanna River, and subsequently with Benjamin Rittenhouse to examine the river Schuylkill. He was also on several occasions called on to serve as commissioner to make treaties with the Indians. On the 27th of June, 1791, he wrote to Governor Mifflin from New Town (now Elmira) that he was there with Colonel Timothy Pickering to meet the Oneida and Onondaga tribes. They were on their way to Painted Post, where the meeting was to be held. About 200 Indians were present to accompany them, but owing to the low water in the river they had given up holding the treaty at Painted Post, and

would see us next morning by Breakfast time in Northumberland. We arrived at the main point at one o'clock. Immediately waited on Colonel Wilson and Dined with him. He informed me that Council in consequence of the application of the Indians Settled on the heads of the Alegina (Allegheny) River and within the Boundareys of Pennsylvania had wrote a letter of Instructions to us of the opinion of Council on the subject of the Indians application; that he expected that the Letter of Instructions would be Brought to hand from Council by Mr. Black; that he thought it would Be improper for us to Proceed without knowing the opinion of Council on these subjects.

This opinion of Mr. Wilson's, I for my own part, intirely agree with. Colonel Matlack spent part of the after noon in cleaning and shooting his gun.

TUESDAY, May 18th.—Mr. Adlum met us in the morning; we agreed to the number of hands necessary for the Expedition; as to the people who were to go with us. Agreed also to purchase some Blankets and other necessarys for the hands. I then Inquired whether Colonel Matlack would wait for the Instructions of Council on the subject of the Indian affairs; he Replyd he would not wait a moment; that they, meaning Council as I apprehended, might send an Express after us with their despatches, if they thought Proper. As I much wanted to see my family I then In-

concluded to hold it at New Town. He also said in the same letter that he was informed that 682 Indians in a body were on their way to meet them. In August, of the same year, he wrote a long letter from Fort Franklin, where he met Cornplanter and other chiefs on public business. He took up much land and at one time possessed many acres. He was a relative of the wife of General Abbot Greene, of Lewisburg. Mr. Adlum settled at Muncy and assisted in making an early map of Pennsylvania. On the 14th of April, 1795, he was appointed by Governor Mifflin one of the first Associate Judges of Lycoming County, and resigned February 16, 1798, on account of contemplated change of residence. He purchased a fine farm near Havre de Grace, Md., and followed farming for several years. His last change of residence was to the District of Columbia, where he died early in the present century. It is regretted that the date of his death is unknown at the present time.

quired when the Boat would leave Northumberland. Mr. Adlum said that he could not go that day, but that the Boat might Proceed as soon as Colonel Matlack Pleased, that he could follow. I then asked Colonel Matlack when he would start from Northumberland; he replied, he thought that afternoon; that they would go up the West Branch five or six miles. I then said that I believed there was nothing further that I could do at that time, that I wished much to see my family.* Colonel Matlack Inquired whether I had got a horse to ride; I informed him that I had and that I wished to go. He agreed and I set off; and him and the Boat Remained at Northumberland for the night.

WEDNESDAY, May 19th.—It appears that Colonel Matlack (was) Detained Last Night in Town in order to Carry Josiah Haner's Goods up to "Darr's" Town† (Lewisburg) where him and one Thornburgh are Erecting a New Store; those goods were on Board and the hands ready to Start by 11 o'clock. As the hands informed me they proceeded with the Boat, came to Mr. T. Rees's where I had Desired that some things for the use of my family might be Landed, and had spoke to Mr. Rees to Receive them, but Colonel Matlack would not suffer them to be Landed, said I might send to Darrs town for them. Mr. Rees told him that he would send his Boy for Mr. Maclay & that he would come down Immediately, but he said he would not wait. At Darrs Town Capt. Lowdon Told Colonel Matlack that Mr. Rees had sent up his son for Mr. Maclay, that he would be Down in a Short time; that Mr. Maclay had waited a week for him in Lebanon. He Re-

---

* Mr. Maclay lived on a farm in Buffalo Valley a short distance West of Lewisburg.

† Originally called Derr's Town, after Ludwig Derr, who lived there as early as 1770. The first survey was made by William Maclay, brother of Samuel, in 1769. The tract was patented on the 11th of August, 1772, to Rev. Richard Peters, who conveyed it to Derr September 17, 1773. It contained 320 acres. Derr laid out the town. March 21, 1812, it was incorporated as a Borough and called Lewisburg.

plyd that he had not, that the time Mr. Maclay waited in Lebanon he had waited on Council and not on him, and that he would not wait one hour on any man and set off with the Boat and hands.

In the mean time I came to Darr's Town Expecting to meet the Boat and Get my Baggage on Board; but it was Gone, and the only account left for me was that they would push as farr as Possible. No alternative was Left; I was obliged to take my Baggage on my Back and follow the Boat, which I did and to ad to the Disagreeable situation in which the Boat left me to shift for my self it Began to Rain, and night came on before I could hear any certain acc't where the Boat had stopped. However, I continued to follow until about 10 o'clock at night, althow the Road was verry Bad and the Night wet and Dark, and found them at James McLaughlin's nearly opposite the mouth of Warrior Run.*

Colonel Matlack's observation to Capt. Lowdon was ill founded. Because the appointment was made with Col. Matlack, not with Council & Matlack had neither wrote or Even sent a Message to Inform Mr. Maclay that a Disapointment had prevented them attending; therefor, Mr. Maclay, if he waited at all, Certainly waited for those Persons with whom he had made the appointment. Another Consideration still Places this matter in a Stronger point of View, Viz., Colonel Matlack called on Council for a much Larger sum of Money than what was agreed on by the commissioners when the appointment was made to meet on the first of May at Lebanon.

THURSDAY, May, 20th.—Rained hard the greater part of the day, which obliged us to continue at McLaughlin's all that day.

FRIDAY, May 21st.—Set off early in the morning. Pushed up about 6 miles where we stopped and Breakfasted & Reached that night, about 2 o'clock, about 2 miles above Wallis's Island.

---

*The thrifty Borough of Watsontown now stands near the mouth of Warrior Run.

SATURDAY, 22d.—Set off; Passed up the Race Ground* Early in the morning; Stopped; Leveled the Race Ground.

Fore Sight 394

Back   "   781
——
387 Difference in 102 perches Distance.

In this place there are 2 large flat Stones and a number of Losse ones, to be Removed which when done Boats can with Ease and Safety be Towed up this place. From thence to Loyal Sock Ripples a fine Easy current.   Loyal Sock Ripples.

Back Sight 915

Fore   "   535
——
380 Difference in 102 perches.

At Loyal Sock we waited some time for Mr. Adlum, and at length set off without him; he overtook (us) in the afternoon, and we took up our camp for the night opposite a small I'ld called Toner's Island. †

SUNDAY, May 23d.—Set off early and the men worked hard all day, and Reached the mouth of the Bald Eagle a little before sunset, where we incamped.

MONDAY, 24th.—Spent the day in Baking Bread, and providing horses for the expedition; Saw Several, but none that suited our purpose.

TUESDAY, May 25th.—The morning threatens Rain; we went

——
*The Race Ground Island, well known to raftsmen, lies in the river about a mile below the mouth of Loyalsock Creek. It was so named because the water runs swiftly around it on the side next Bald Eagle Mountain. It always was a dangerous place for raftsmen, and many rafts have been wrecked on the head of the island, as the water in rushing around to the right side, or channel, is treacherous and requires great care on the part of pilots to avoid being drawn on the bar.

† A small island in the river opposite the present town of Linden. The water has encroached upon it very much and it is almost entirely washed away.

and Breakfasted with Mrs. Don.* Looked at several horses but could not buy any that we thought Exactly suited our purpose; we at length purchased three, and left Gersham Hicks and Mathew Gray to get them Shod, and prepared to start with the Boat.

WEDNESDAY, May 26th.—Started with the Boat, and found it Good Boatable water up as far as Tangascutack,† but between that and Baker's there were a number of Ripples and Sholes, which took up so much time that it was nearly night when the Boat arrived there where we encamped for the night.

THURSDAY, May 27th.—Started Early and arrived at Bennet's before sun set. In this day's push we found much difficulty occasioned by Ripples & Sholes.

FRIDAY, May 28th.—Set off and Passed through several Sholes and one sharp Ripple, and about 1 o'clock came to Shin Town‡ where we spent the Remainder of the Day in Baking & Cooking.

SATURDAY, May 29th.—Breakfasted and set off. I this morning felt much out of order; the Evening before after I drank tea, I was taken with a severe pain in my Left arm, Which I took for an attack of Rheumatism, but in a short time it Removed from my arm and fixed in my Breast, and continued Very Painful at night. We had not Traveled far before it began to Rain; we, however, kept moving Slowly along; we met with some sharp Ripples and some Sholes, but the sholes we had this day were not as bad as those between Shin Town & the young women's§ town. We ar-

---

*She resided on the Great Island, which her husband, William Dunn—according to tradition—purchased from the Indians "for a barrel of whiskey, a rifle and a hatchet." It contained about 300 acres and was a favorite place of resort for the aborigines. It lies in the river a short distance east of Lock Haven.

† A small stream emptying into the river two miles west of Farrandsville. Coal was formerly mined on this stream.

‡ A hamlet a short distance above Renovo. At that time it could not have been more than a cabin.

§ The village of North Point is now located at the mouth of Youngwoman's Creek.

rived at the mouth of the Sinnemahoning River* about 1 o'clock, and proceeded up the River about one mile and a half, and encamped. It still Continued Raining.

SUNDAY, May 30th.—Proceeded up the Cinamahoning with the Boat, Got up the falls† without much Difficulty. In them there are a few Stones that appear to be loose, that must be removed, that may be don for about £10. We got about 3¼ (miles) further up to the point of an island, where is a shole, when we were obliged to put out about half our loading, and then got up with the Boat and proceeded up the River about 3¼ of a mile, unloaded the Boat, and sent her back for that part we had left at the Ripple. As soon as she returned we got our load on board and pushed up the River about half a mile, where we meet with another shole, which we could not pass. We then pushed our boat a little back and encamped for the night. About Dark it thundered, and in the night it rained a little; and though we had near three days of cloudy weather and some rain, the river continued to fall.

MONDAY, May 31st.—The morning cloudy with a misty rain. About 8 o'clock it cleared up, then all hopes of the river rising at the time were ended. We then, as the last resource, set James McLaughlin with 4 other hands to work to make us canoes.‡ After this was agreed on Mr. Adlum and myself set off, and climbed to the top of a mountain § that lay to the northeast of our camp and came close to the river. As we passed along its foot, (it) did not appear high, but when we attempted climbing it, we found it a verry high mountain, and the country to the north appeared to be

---

* Now called Keating. At this point the West Branch runs from the southwest, and the Sinnemahoning, which empties into it, runs from the west.

† The Moccasin Falls. This name was given to the falls by the Indians.

‡ These canoes were evidently made near what is known as the Round Island. The name was given to it because rafts could pass around it on either side.

§ This mountain is supposed to be the high peak lying northeast of the First Fork at the village of Sinnemahoning. Hon. John Brooks, civil engineer, says its summit is 1,900 feet above tide.

pretty level, and the soil of a middlin quality. We traveled about 2 or 3 miles and then came down the mountain to the river about 2 miles below our camp. We on our way took up McLaughlin's Broad ax which had been forgot the day before, where we loaded our boat after getting up the ripples. We got to camp about 2 o'clock. After dinner colonel Matlack and Mr. Adlum walked up to see how the canoe making came on, and I assisted the boys at Baking Bread. This with a dish of tea concluded the month of May.

TUESDAY, June 1st, 1790.—The hands were employed in working at our canoes and baking Bread. Mr. Adlum and myself walked down the river near three miles, but met with no game. Returned, Got Dinner and then walked up to see the canoe making.

WEDNESDAY, June 2d.—Spent the fornoon in Lineing the River up as far as our camp. About 1 o'clock one of our canoes was launced, but I have not yet seen here since she was put in the water.

THURSDAY, June 3d.—Loaded our canoe and proceeded up the river, Surveying it as we went; we surveyed it up as far as the second fork, where we arrived about 4 o'clock. We spent the remainder of the day in pitching our tent and unloading our canoe, and unpacking some of our stores which had got wet.

FRIDAY, June 4th.—In the morning sent off James Carney and Edward Sweney with the canoe to go back to where we had left James McLaughlin and the other hands to finish the other canoe. Carney and Sweney were ordered to return this day with another Load of our stores, but are not yet Returned.

Carney and Sweney Returned in the evening and brought with them a small load of stores.

SATURDAY, June 5th.—Sent of Saml Gibbons and Matthew Gray in the morning early for another load; they returned at 2 o'clock, unloaded the canoe and set off for the old camp in order to bring the remainder of our stores. On the way they met McLaughlin and Reynolds with the new canoe loaded, on their way.

SUNDAY, June 6th.—McLaughlin and Reynolds had come part of the way on Saturday and came to camp at 10 o'clock, and Brought with them a large she Beaver, that McLaughlin had caught at 2 small islands* that are about a mile below the first forks. At one o'clock the other canoe with the Remainder of our Stores arrived; the Residue of the day was spent in preparing provisions, Packing tents, etc.

MONDAY, June 7th.—The canoes were Loaded and all hands set forward with them, Hicks and myself Excepted. I chused to stay with Hicks in consequence of my having been much indisposed for the two Preceeding days, as Hicks had to take care of the horses and make pack saddles; I amused myself in assisting him; I still felt Rather unwell; some remains of my head ach continued with a pain or rather soreness cross my kidneys.

Mr. Adlum with three hands intends to run a line cross the canoeing place to the Alegina,† and get some of our people set to work at making our canoes on the Alegina. Before he returns to this camp, as soon as that can be accomplished, we intend to survey the West Branch as high as it will admit canoes, and then examine what kind of communication the country will admit of Between it and Toby's Creek. ‡

At night Hicks was taken with a cold fit which lasted about a quarter of an hour, and then complained of a hard lump in his stomach, and Likewise that his stomach was sick. He drank water and vomited and then the chillness together with the sickness went off. I caught as many chub in a short time, at the junction of the two branches, as made our supper.

---

* Believed to be what are known to-day as the "Grass Flat Islands," a short distance below the present town of Sinnemahoning.

† The Allegheny River west of the mountains of that name.

‡ Now called the Clarion River.

TUESDAY, June 8th.—Hicks and myself Bussey in finishing our Pack Saddles. This morning we saw a deer in the River coming to a small Island; I immediately went after it; but could see no more of it this day. Likewise be it remembered that I made a Plumb Pudding in a Bag at the second forks of the Sinemahoning,* and had it for dinner, and thought it as fine a one as I ever ate. A slight showr this evening, but not sufficient to raise the River; about 5 o'clock a canoe with two men and two boys, came to our camp; they said they had come from Pine Creek in four days. They discovered an inclination to stay all night at our fire, without either being invited or asking leave; their conversation was of hunting, and though in general fond of hearing hunting Feats, they in order to appear Singular made themselves Exceedingly disagreeable. I have not yet learned any of their names, and if they would push their Boats I would feel more happy than either their company or acquaintance could make me.

WEDNESDAY, June 9th.—My disagreeable guests were gone this morning before I got up. Got Breakfast; shot my gun at a mark; saw a large wolf Crossing the Left hand branch about 150 yards above our camp; hearing the guns fired he, I suppose, expected either to find the offall of some game or find some game wounded. The time is now arrived at which I expect the return of our canoes, 3 o'clock; 4 o'clock, the canoes returned; the men complained that they were fatigued; (in) order that they might rest a little, I undertook to bake some bread. They in the mean time took the canoes out of the water, and made fires under their Bottoms to Dry them, that they might run lighter and carry a greater Burthen. Last night McLaughlin caught a second Beaver, and so the day concluded with cooking and the other usual avocations.

THURSDAY, June 10th.—The morning rained until about 9 o'clock; in the time of the rain Thomas Semor† came up to our

---

*Now known as the borough of Driftwood.

† Seymour, properly.

camp. As soon as the Rain began to abate I ordered the hands to begin to put our Baggage on Board and Got ready as quick as Possible and set off. As our canoes were unable to take all our baggage along, in the State the water was, I put our tent and several other things on Board of Semor's canoe, and went on Board with him & told him that he should be paid a reasonable compensation for his trouble. We were as Diligent as possible until night, and were only able to get eight miles that day; the water was so low that we were obliged to Drag our canoes through every ripple, and in Several of them were obliged to Quarrey a passage through for our canoes.

FRIDAY, June 11th.—Rose early, had the Breakfast Got Ready as soon as Possible, and started this morning. I felt myself unable to work in the canoe with Semor; I have felt the Rheumatism for several days in my right arm and sholder, and the workin the Preceding day had increased my pain. I continued on shore alone until about one o'clock, and then Expecting that the heavy canoes could not reach the uper camp that day, I got my Blanket put on Board of Semor's Light canoe, and desired him to push on for the uper camp, and I kept along shore with him for some time, when finding the water to get worse, and not being in condition to give him much assistance, I determined to walk on to the upper camp. I did so and Reach(ed) the place about 5 o'clock. Hicks, who had brought the horses, got there a few minutes before me; him, I sent back to assist Semor in Bringing up his Canoe. They returned with the Canoe Before sunset. I need scarcely ad that I was Sufficiently Fatigued to go to Bed early.

SATURDAY, June 12th.—Sent Hicks and Semor off early this morning with Semor's canoe to meet the other Canoes and to take a part of their loads, and to assist in Bringing them up. They met them about 2 miles Below the camp and took a part of their loads and returned with them. In about 3 hours it began to rain and now Rains pretty fast; Mr. Adlum not yet returned.

SUNDAY, June 13th.—After Breakfast Began to Bake Bread in Expectation that Mr. Adlum and his party would return Early in the day from their Excursion to the Alegina; waited in that Expectation until 12 o'clock, then as the Branch had rose in consequence of the Rain, it was determined that I should take the advantage of the rising of the water and Proceed to Explore and survey the other Branch of Sinemahoning and run a line from the canoe place on the west Branch to connect with Little Toby's Creek, and not wait longer for Mr. Adlum's return. The hand(s) alloted for this Expedition were Thomas Semor, Gersham Hicks and Matthew Gray. I then got ten day's Provisions for four hands put on Board the Canoes, and went my self on board, with Semor, Hicks and Gray on Board of our long canoe which was to be left at the forks. We proceeded down the creek when upon enquiry I found the hands had forgot to bring salt with them; I then ordered Mathew Gray to Run Back to camp for some salt, and Hicks to wait for him and told Hicks that we would let our canoe float until they would overtake us. We floated on until we came five miles, then we waited until the knats and musketoes grew too Troublesom; I then told Semor that we would Get on board and proceed down the creek to the camp where we had lodged as we went up, and kindle a fire and then wait for Hicks & Gray.

We set off, came to our old camp, Kindled fire, provided firewood and prepared for the night, but still no word from Hicks & Gray. A thousand conjectures presented themselves. At length Hicks* came before it grew quite dark; he had waited for Gray's return until he thought he had time to have come back, and as he did not come within the time that he allowed him he came without him. This accident Triffling as it may seem, was really imberasing. I knew not what to do, nor could I do anything. It was night in a country where there were no roads. I had however

---

* Hicks was an early settler on Bennett's Branch, near the mouth of Hicks' Run, which was named after him. He was half Indian.

some hope that Gray when he came back to where he had left Hicks and the canoe, and saw that they were Gone, would Hurey along in order to overtake the canoe, and that if he was unable to reach my fire that night, he would be with us early in the morning. In that Expectation I went to Sleep.

MONDAY, June 14th.—Early, I ordered Hicks to put some chocolate on to boyl in order to have Breakfast ready should Gray have come in, according to my expectation; waited for some time, then took breakfast; still no account of Gray, the creek falling, the favorable opportunity for which I had waited steeling away, and I by this accident toatally prevented from prosecuting my intended journey. I then sent off Semor and Hicks in the light canoe in order to see what was become of Gray; as I write I hear the canoe poles Returning. They are returned and have brought in Gray, so now we are preparing to proceed to the forks. We arrived there about 12 o'clock; Immediately got ready and began to survey the west branch * of the Sinemahoning and got a little way above Boyd's whetstone Quarrey † before night having surveyed the creek 6 miles and 23 perches. Encamped for the night.

* Better known to-day as Bennett's Branch, which falls into the Sinnemahoning at Driftwood. There the two streams uniting form what is properly known as the Sinnemahoning River, which unites with the West Branch of the Susquehanna at Keating, twelve miles below. Bennett's Branch was formerly called the "Second Fork." The Driftwood branch is called the main stream, because it has several large tributaries, viz.: The Portage, West Creek, North Creek, &c. It was on these streams where the Commissioners spent so much time surveying. Bennett's Branch was named after John Bennett, who went there from what is now Lycoming County about 1785. Erasmus Morey, of Benezett, now in his 92d year, says that Bennett's main cabin was near the mouth of Trout Run, at Benezett. When he (Morey) located there in 1814 the corn hills, cultivated by Bennett, were still visible. He was quite a farmer for that time and yoked his cows to do the plowing. He also had another cabin near the mouth of the branch, a short distance above the present borough of Driftwood.

† Hon. John Brooks, of Sinnemahoning, who has resided there for nearly 70 years, says that the Whetstone quarry was at the Moccasin Falls, about two miles above the mouth of the Sinnemahoning, and ten miles below Driftwood. Whetstones are found there in the cliffs on the north side of the Sinnemahoning. The quarry is no longer worked. Erasmus Morey says that at an early day there was

TUESDAY, June 15th.—Began my survey early in the morning and continued with all Possable Diligence until about 5 o'clock, when we arrived at old Mr Bennet's cabbin, three quarters of a mile above the forks; we then took up our camp for the night.

WEDNESDAY, June 16th.—Spent the morning until Breakfast in Transcribing the notes of the two preceeding days, and as soon as I had finished them began my survey of the Branch. We this day had great difficulty in getting our canoe taken up as the water was verrey low above the first fork of the Branch. I was often obliged to wait for Semor and the canoe, and send the chain carriers to assist him, which lost me so much time that I was only able to get about 6 miles up the Branch when we incamped. The difficulty of the Business are fast increasing & our Provisions fast decreasing, and I find myself much fatigued.

THURSDAY, June 17th.—The morning cloudy and some rain, though not enough to raise the water for us. We must however proceed as there is no saving provision in the woods, and though there is some appearance of game in the country, yet we have got nothing. We set (off) and continued our survey by corse and distance up to the second forks; further than that we could not take our canoe. We were then obliged with our canoe to leave the most part of our Baggage; I left two of my Blankets, shoes and stockings. Took one blanket on my back which with the instrument made my load. The men who had to carry their own baggage and the provision could not measure, encumbered as they were. I was therefore obliged to quit it, and carried the instrument in my hand; took the courses of the creek and estimated the distance. In this manner I proceeded up the creek about a mile and a half making in the whole 4 miles since we left our canoe, when Semor who had got a little distance ahead Shot at a

a place on Bennett's Branch called "Whetstone Narrows," below Hicks' Run, where whetstones and grindstones were made. He says that Boyd built the first saw mill on Bennett's Branch in the summer of 1816.

Doe Elk. We came up to where he had left his load and made a halt; in the mean time we heard the Doe calling her fawn. Hicks then went over the creek to look for the Doe & after he was gone some time Semor shot a second time; Hicks in that instant started the fawn; it Run back to the creek and came within shot; I shot and killed it on the spot. Semor came back and said he had wounded the Doe, and him and Hicks went after it with the Dog; the dog in a short time drove another fawn into the creek just by where I stod. My gun was emty; Indeed I wished the fawn to Escape, But the dog caught it and him and Matthew Gray had a frolick with it Indeed. Semor and Hicks returned but found not the Doe. I then ordered a fire and the Kettle to be put on and Determined to stay and feast for the night.

FRIDAY, June 18th.—The mountains smoky and the appearance of rain. We however set off after an Early Breakfast, and traveled on until about one o'clock when we were stoped by a shower; after it left off Raining Proceeded on, until near sundown when we stopt and began to make a camp, as there was the appearance of a Gust. We had not got our camp finished when the rain began; there was just a moderate shower, though from the appearance as the shower came up I had expected a very heavy shower.

SATURDAY, June 19th.—As the Bushes were wet with Rain we staid at our camp untill after we had got Breakfast and then set off and walked the Branch about 2½ miles where the Branch forks. We took up the north fork, and travelled up nearly south about half a mile and came to the Big Elk lick,* there were two Doe elks in the lick at one of which my gun missed fire at the distance

---

* The lick mentioned here evidently was not the "great lick" on the Portage Creek. There was a large lick and several smaller ones in the Trout Run region. There was a lick near the mouth of Trout Run, and in after years Stephen Winslow manufactured salt there. Salt was also manufactured at Driftwood from 1810 to 1819. A well 65 feet deep was sunk and the salt water pumped up. John Jordan was one of the early settlers there in 1806. The party operating the salt works was known as the Lycoming Salt Company. Judge Burnside was one of the owners, and a man named Webb was president.

of 50 yards. We then took up a point of the mountain along what
we supposed to be an Elk path but soon found new and old Indian
marks along it. As soon as I reached the top of the hill, I took
out the instrument and took the corse to the uper forks of the
Creek of which I had a tolarable Distinct view, and found that we
were nearly N. W. from the forks and about 4½ or five miles
Distant.

Hicks and Semor then set the compass to strike Toby's creek
and agreed in the corse; the corse the set was N. 14 W., But as
the Indian path was newly marked, and, as we supposed by the
Indians whose marks we had seen at several places along Sinemahoning, and as we expected that they had come from Toby's Creek
it was thought advisable to follow the path. It took nearly a northeast Corse; we followed it about three miles. I then concluded
that it went to the heads of the other Branch of Sinemahoning;
we then took the woods and set off at N. 14 W., but soon found
that it was impossible to keep a corse between brush of every Description, fallen timber and Rocks. We were obliged to pick our
way more antious for our own safety than keeping our course. We
traveled on keeping our corse as well as we could for about 4
miles, when we crossed a small branch or rather run that falls into
Toby's creek; we had not gone far this corse which was nearly
west before we crossed Shearer's north line. We (had) verrey bad
walking but kept at it with Diligence until about 5 o'clock, when
we reached Toby's at the little Elk lick about three miles below
where Shearers north line stricks Toby's creek. I found the corse
of Toby's where I was along it to be about S. W. which corse it
keeps for about 3 miles further and then turns nearly north, which
corse it keeps untill it falls into Big* Toby's creek, and appears to
be adapted for inland navigation.

SUNDAY, June 20th.—Left our Camp on Little Toby's creek
after we had Breakfasted, and set off in a south east direction,

---

*Near the present borough of Ridgway, the capital of Elk County.

which direction we followed as near as circumstances would permit but were by Brush and fallen Timber obliged to turn Considerable more to the East, and came to the Indian path about a mile N. E. of the Big Elk Lick on the Sinemahoning. The Ground Between the Sinemahoning and Little Toby's Creek is a Barren mountain; in some places covered with a poor stunted Grouth of Pitch pine, but the far greater part of the mountain has some years ago been covered with small chestnut timber, which has been killed with fire and is now fallen, and the underwood is grown up among (it) so thick that in many places it fairly hid the logs, which makes walking both Dangerous and Difficult.

The distance between the Elk lick or the head of the upermost North East Branch of Sinemahoning, and Little Toby's Creek Dos not Exceed Seven miles in a N. W. Direction, and the Country will admit of a Good road; the only difficulty, or at least the great one, will be making the Road up the South Side of the mountain; and in case a road should Ever be attempted in that part the Best and Easiest place is the end of the Ridge or spur, below the lick.   When I returned to the waters of Sinemahoning, though I had not travelled a great Distance, yet I felt fatigued, and Encamped.

MONDAY, June 21st.—We were obliged to spend part of this morning in Baking some bread.   While this was doing I walked about 1½ miles to a Elk lick; I much wished to kill one as our fresh meat was done, but I saw none.   I returned, and as soon as the Baking was compleated, we started.   We then had only one day's allowance of Bread, no more flour; and were 50 miles at least, the way we had to go, from our General camp.   These circumstances induced me to make as much haste as possible.   I walked all Day, though in much pain with my Rheumatick complaints, and got to within three miles of where we had left our canoe as we went up; there I incamped for the night, much Fatigued.

TUESDAY, June 22d.—Our supper the Preceeding Day had finished our Bread; we had two Squares of Chocolate left, and a remnant of sugar, Some Bacon; but neither Bread nor flour. We set off & came to our canoe; found her & everything we had left safe. Semor, one of the hands I had with me, had a little Indian meal which he had left along with our tent and other things. Upon this meal we got to work, made some Dumplings and Boiled them in our Chocolate, and made with the addition of a slice of Bacon, a very hearty Breakfast. Put our things on board; Hicks and I started to go before to an Elk lick,* in hops of Getting some meat, and left Tho's Semor and Matthew Gray to Bring the Canoe with the Baggage. Hicks and I were again unsucksessful, we saw none. My feet were by this time so sore that walking was verrey painful. I was obliged to go on Board the Canoe, though the water was so low that the men were obliged to Drag the Canoe one third of the way. We arrived at Bennet's Cabbin about the middle of the afternoon. There was then great appearance of rain, and in our situation, the raising of the water only a few inches would have been of vast consequence and as we had still a little of the Indian meal, I concluded to stay there that night, & Bake the meal and Boil a part of the Gammon which we had, concluding that if a rain should come as there was great appearance of it, we would gain time rather than Loos, as, by having our provision all cooked we would have nothing to delay us the next day.

WEDNESDAY, June 23d.—Set off from Bennet's Cabbin Early in the morning, and got down to the forks about the middle of the afternoon. At the point I left six small whetstones and a large piece of the same kind of stone for James McLaughlin to carry with for me to Buffaloe. As the water in the North Branch was verrey low, we Left our Tent in order to lighten our canoe, and without any delay we proceeded up the North Branch putting Hicks and Gray aboard of the canoe, and Semor and I walked.

---

* At the mouth of Trout Run, where the town of Benezett is now located.

We got about four miles up the Branch and encamped a little before sun set.

THURSDAY, June 24th.—Started in the morning and reached our uper camp about 3 o'clock. About half an hour after I got there, Mr. Adlum arrived from our camp on the Ohia,* a Branch or rather the head of the Alegina river, and brought us an account that James McLaughlin had finished two canoes there for us and was on his way returning; but had the misfortune to cut his foot with the adze.

FRIDAY, June 25th.—It rained in the night and in the morning it continued to rain. James McLaughlin and Reynolds came to Camp about 10 o'clock, and Began immediately to prepair to return home. By them I wrote a line to Mrs Maclay and James McLaughlin promised to send the Letter by a safe hand to Mrs Maclay; he likewise promised to take with him a large piece of whetstone from the forks which I left there and one small Elk horn and a piece of a large one. We took some pains to put Jimmey in good humor before he left us, but he seemed to part with us rather in Dudgen. I likewise left 6 small whetstones, which I brought from Boyd's Quarrey.

SATURDAY, June 26th.—Mr. Adlum with two hands set out after Breakfast to survey the Road between our Camp on the North Branch of Sinemahoning and the new camp on the Alegina.† After he started Colonel Matlack and myself took a walk up the Branch, as far as a mile above the second forks that were above our camp. At the first fork ‡ the Left hand Branch coms from the south, and the other from the N. W., and the water nearly equal in both. At the

---

* Either on Portage or Potato Creek, near where the town of Port Allegany now stands.

† At or near the Portage, as it was called, because the Indians carried their light canoes overland to the waters of the Allegheny.

‡ The village of Sinnemahoning is located here. When Col. Matlack and Mr. Maclay were here on the 26th of June, 1790, there were no white settlers in this section. It was a very wild place—in fact a "howling wilderness."

second forks the Left hand branch comes partly from the west, and the other from the N. W. or rather more to the north; the Left hand Branch here has near Twist as much water as the Right. Up the right are two Elk licks. A heavy rain wet us to the skin before we returned.

SUNDAY, June 27th.—Spent a verrey disagreeable night; had a most voilent Tooth ach which continued all Day to be verrey Troublesome.

MONDAY, June 28th.—Had another distressing night. Face much swelled in the morning, and yet the pain in my tooth continues.

TUESDAY, June 29th.—Suffered much last night with a head ach. My face continues swelled; I'm altogether unwell. We expect our pack horses to return this day by 12 o'clock.

WEDNESDAY, June 30th.—Felt something Better. Got all our Baggage Packed up and Loaded & at 10 o'clock set off; and that, and Got onwards about 9 mile. Passed the Large salt lick * and encamped for the night.

THURSDAY, July 1st.—Started early, and reached our camp on the

---

*The "Great Elk Lick," as it was called by the old hunters, was located here. It was probably the largest in the world, and was on what is now known as the line of the Buffalo, New York and Philadelphia Railroad, near the station called Shippen. It was about ten miles north of Emporium. A short distance south is Sizerville, now attracting much attention on account of the medicinal properties of the water obtained there through a flowing well. The stream running south here is the Portage branch (of the Driftwood branch) of the Sinnemahoning, which empties into the Driftwood at Emporium. This salt or elk lick is mentioned in John Hanna's notes of the survey of the lands of the Holland Land Company, made by him in 1793. In his notes he speaks of beginning a block of surveys about 4½ miles north of the "Big Elk Lick," on the line of survey made by John Adlum. The lick was very large. The ground around it for at least three acres was literally cleared of brush by the stamping herds of elk and deer. Old hunters used to relate that they had seen as high as thirty elk in the lick at one time, and hundreds were killed there. What was afterwards known as the "Salt Works," or "Parker Salt Well," occupied its site. This section of the State, embracing Potter, McKean and Elk counties, and what is now Cameron County, was the last retreat of the elk. As late as 1841 a herd of thirteen still existed in these forests, but they were slain one by one until the species became extinct.

Ohia about 3 o'clock; found none of our people at camp but Hicks. Mr. Adlum had set off in the morning to survey the River Down to the State line.* The remaining part of the day I spent in assisting in Launcing our canoes, and in writing to my son Billey.

FRIDAY, July 2d.—Loaded our canoes and proceeded down the Ohia; met with considerable difficulty in getting along over the shoales, the River Being too Low. About 12 o'clock met two Indians, one of which called himself Doctor Thomas. These Indians, as they informed us, had been sent up from the Town by the Cheiff, to see if we were comming down, and when we would be there. We traveled together until night, and Encamped together.

SATURDAY, July 3d.—Set off in the morning and had Tolerable water. Reached the State Line at 3 o'clock, where we found Mr. Adlum and his party. The Indians still continued with us; as we had Bread to Bake we concluded to stay there all night, and set off Early in the morning, and go to the town, the Doctor chusing to stay with us for the night, and his companion with him although we had desired him to go to the Town, and inform their Cheiff, that we intended to be at the town in the morning.

SUNDAY, July 4th.†—Set off Early in the morning and made the best of our way to the Town. The Indians started a little Before us, and as their canoe was a Light one, they reached the Town a considerable time Before us. We got to the town at 9 o'clock, went down Below the town a little Distance; we kindled a fire and got our Breakfast. Several of the Indians came to our fire, but the principal man was out of town, and it seemed that we must wait

---

* The Allegheny River, which has its source in Potter County, flows northward into the State of New York. It then makes a great bend to the left like a horseshoe, and enters the State of Pennsylvania again, when it runs southwestwardly to the Ohio. When the Commissioners were there they regarded it as the Ohio proper.

† Attention is called to the fact that the Fourth of July, 1790, came on Sunday. The Republic was then just fourteen years old, but it seems that the Commissioners did not "celebrate."

for him.   We waited until the afternoon, and were then given to understand that Con-ne-Shangon, their Cheif was Gon to Vanango, But a certain Captain John supplyd his place.   He made us a speech in the afternoon to the following Effect: That him and all their men Returns thanks to almighty God for the oppertunity of Speaking to his Brothers, that as he now speaks he hopes that you will hear; that you are come to poor people, that are all suffering. Another thing he hopes; that he knew nothing of our coming until he Looked up and saw us come Down the water; he hopes that we will take pitty on their women and children and give them something to prevent them from starving.

MONDAY, July 5th.—Set off in the morning, two Indians Gowin with us, viz: Capt John and 10 Days; and the doctor on hors Back. About the middle of the afternoon we came to an Indian Camp on shore where the(y) had whiskey, which they offred us; at this camp we saw a Duchman who in the war had been taken Prisoner and it seem(s) chused to continue with the Indians.   We delayed but a short time at this camp; we put on and Left the Indians. After some time the Indians came up with us & the Doctor had got himself a little Drunk, just so much as to put him to show his horsmanship, and in attempting to ride up a steep Bank him and his horse tumbled together into the River.   We took up our camp a little before sunset &c.

TUESDAY, July 6th.—Took our Breakfast and set off and came to Tuis-In-Guis-an-Gothtaw* about 10 o'clock.   We soon found that the Doctor who had reached the town before us had been doing us Ill offices with the people of the town.   They looked remarkable sour, and insisted on our stoping until they could send for their cheif the Cornplanter who lived about 7 miles below, at a place called Jen Oh Show Dego.†   We said that we could go on

---

*Supposed to be the Indian town of *Tiozinosongochto,* as laid down on the Historical Map of Pennsylvania.   It was in what is now Potter County, near the McKean line.

†Given on the Historical Map of Pennsylvania as *Jeane Sedago.*

and call on the Cornplanter, where he lived. They said no; it was not manly to call about Busness at a Cabbin in the woods, and said that they had a hold of the stern of our canoe; plainly intimating that the(y) could and would make us stay.

We thought it best to be as accomading as we could, and told them to send for the Cornplanter and we would stay untill the afternoon. About noon their cheif came and told us that he had sent for the Cornplanter; that he expected him soon, but that we must not think the time Long. His advise had no effect for we did think the day a verrey Long one. Night came at last but no Cornplanter.

WEDNESDAY, July 7th.—The Cornplanter came about 8 o'clock and appeared to be friendly disposed; said he would look for a place where we might meet and speak to each other. We met, Told our Busness, and delivered the Cornplanter his letter which was read, and Interpretated to the Indians by one Matthews. They then all appeared in good humor; and the Cornplanter in a speech told us he was glad to see us, and gave us a welcom to anything we could catch in their country. Then we were addressed by an Oritor in behalf of the wemon. They told us that they were Glad to see us, that they hoped we were well, that we had come a long road, that they had heard the good news we had brought, that they thought that as the severest part of the labour of living fell to their Lot, they had a right to Speak and to be heard, and again thanked us for our Good News, that they hoped that as soon as the Good Road we had spoke of was made, they would be able to purchase what things they wanted on Better terms.

True their Trade at this time was much worse than formerly owing to the Scarcity of Game, but that if a good Road was made it would still be worth while for Traders to come among them and that they hoped a Good Corespondence would still be cultivated between them and us untill we should become one people. Their speech was answered verrey Properly by Col'l Matlack; as soon as that was Ended though it rained we Got on Board of our Canoes and pushed Down the River, and took up our camp oposite Capt'n Jno. Obeal's Town* and had the honor of his Company at supper.

THURSDAY, July 8th.—The morning rainy; after Breakfast it cleared, it cleared and Mr Adlum went up to the State line to survey the river & to assist me in making a Survey for the Cornplanter. This Busness kept us Imployed until about 4 o'clock; as we were Both wet when we came to camp we concluded to stay where we were for the night.

---

*This was the residence of Cornplanter, a distinguished Seneca Chief. His Indian name was Gy-ant-wa-chia, but among the English he was known as Abeel, O'Beal and O'Bail. The latter is correct according to the testimony of Mary Jemison. In the Indian language his town was called *Tenachshegonchtongee,* or the burnt house. When Colonel Proctor visited it, in 1791, he found the town pleasantly situated on the north side of the river and containing twenty-eight tolerably good houses or cabins. Cornplanter's father was a white man named O'Bail, and according to Stone, in his Life of Brant (Vol. II., p. 121), he was in the habit of traveling back and forth from Albany through the Seneca country, to Niagara, as a trader. Becoming enamored of a pretty squaw among the Senecas, in process of time the Cornplanter became one of the living evidences of his affection. When he grew to manhood and became a leader in his tribe he was not ignorant of his origin. Stone says that he sent a party of warriors to capture his father and bring him before him. On his arrival he informed the old man that he knew that he was his father, but he should not be harmed. If he chose to remain with him and adopt the manners and customs of his tribe, he would take care of him; if not, he would be allowed to depart in peace. The old man departed. Cornplanter figured prominently in the Indian wars. He was a contemporary of Washington and was at Braddock's defeat. He was one of the negotiators and signers to the treaties of Fort Stanwix and Fort Harmar. Once won over from the French, he maintained his allegiance to the English faithfully during the Indian war from 1790 to 1794, rendering valuable assistance to the general government and in the protection of the western frontiers of Pennsylvania. For these services, among other rewards, he received from Pennsylvania permission to select 1,500 acres of land from unappropriated territory for himself and his posterity. He chose for his own occupancy a tract of 640 acres on the Allegheny River, 14 miles above Warren. Here he located about 1790 and lived there until his death in 1836, at the age of one hundred or upwards, and here his descendants still live to the number of about seventy-five. In 1866 the Legislature authorized the erection of a monument to his memory, which was done under the direction of Samuel P. Johnson, Esq., of Warren, at a cost of $550. Three of his children were present at the dedication, the last of whom died in 1874, at the age of about 100 years.—*History of Pennsylvania, Egle,* p. 1135.

FRIDAY, July 9th.—Set off after Breakfast, and proceeded down River to the mouth of the Kinjua* where we parted with Mr Adlum; he proceeded up the Kinjua with two of the hand(s), accompanied with an Indian called Tim I Tugmutton. We proceeded Down the River to the mouth of the Cannowango † and Got up the same about 2 miles, where we incamped for the night.

SATURDAY, July 10th.—In the morning Proceeded up the Connowango about 2 miles further where we Left one of our canoes & all our Baggage that we could spare in the care of Sam'l Gibbons, takin with us only Provisions for 10 Days, and set off for the Jadockque Lake,‡ having one Mathews with us to act as an Interpretor, as we expected to met with several Indians. We kept with Deligence at the poles & Paddles all Day, and Got 17 miles as we computed.

SUNDAY, July 11th.—We started in the morning and kept steadyly at work all day, and made as we computed 17 miles further up the Cannowango. In these 2 days Traveling, with our canoes, we had not more than 10 miles of strong watter, the Rest of the River being lik a mill Pond, and in the General so deep that we could not find the Bottom with our setting poles. For the shape of the River see paper numbred 2.

MONDAY, July 12th.—Set of(f) in the morning, and found it Extreamly Difficult to get up the creek; the water was verrey Low and Divided with a great number of small Islands, and the channels stoped up with Drift wood and timber that had fallen cross the creek. In some places we cleared a passage; in others we were obliged to Slide our canoe on Scates. We had about five miles of

---

*The Kinzua, which empties into the Allegheny River twelve miles above Warren.

† The Conewango Creek, which falls into the Allegheny at Warren, is the outlet of Chautauqua Lake.

‡ Chautauqua Lake, in the State of New York, now such a popular place of resort.

this kind of water; at length we entered the Jadockque Lake*
which for about 2 miles widned Gradually. The Shores Remarkably muddy and covered with Splater Docks. From thence the
lake opens at wonst, and has a verrey Pleasing appearance. We
got about 4 miles up and encamped.

TUESDAY, July 13th.—Set off after Breakfast; the morning per-
fectly calm and the whole face of the Lake as far as the Eye could
see, as smooth as Glass; the country beyond the Lake Rose Gradually, and was covered entirely with oak, now in Bloom. This
with the Lake formed as Pleasing a Prospect as I ever Saw. We
stude up the Lake to what we supposed was the head of it; when
we had reached the part we took for its western point, we found it
only a narrow point of Land that shote into the Lake, and found
that we still had the Greater part of the Lake before us. We
made all the speed, we possably could and at one o'clock we got
within a mile of the head of the Lake. We there went on shore
and cooke(d) a pike we had shote that was three feet three inches
Long, for our Dinner. After Dinner went round the head of the
Lake and down the west side a Little Distance, where Colonel
Matlack and I went on Shore in search of the Road to Lake Erie;
we found it in a little time, and returned to our Canoe. Went a
little further Down the Lake and encamped.

---

*The lake is located in Chautauqua County, New York, about eight miles
south of the eastern end of Lake Erie. It is a little over sixteen miles long, is
1,291 feet above tide water and 726 feet higher than Lake Erie. Its outlet issues
from the southeastern end and enters Conewango Creek, which empties into the
Allegheny River at Warren. Chautauqua, which is spelled "Shatakoin," "Jad-
achque," "Cahdocin," "Chauddauk-wa" and "Jah-dah-quah," by the early French
writers, is said to mean "a place where a child was swept away by the waves,"
"where a fish was taken out," "the foggy place, &c." La Salle is supposed to
have been the first white man to visit the lake, in August, 1669. Celoron followed, with a body of troops and Indians, in July, 1749. He explored the lake,
and then descended through Conewango Creek to the Allegheny, where he buried
a leaden plate signifying that he had taken possession of the country in the name
of the King of France. When the French established a line of forts across the
country to Pittsburg, Chautauqua Lake was one of their important points. They
built a road connecting it with Lake Erie, over which they transported their
troops, provisions and munitions of war.

WEDNESDAY, July 14th.—In the morning Colonel Matlack, my-self and two hands Got Redy with two days Provision, and set off on the old French Road to Lake Erie. We were able to travel the Road without difficulty. In many places the Cart Ruts were verrey plain. We walke(d) on in high Spirits untill Between Ten and Eleven o'clock when we were met by a Verrey heavy Rain, which lasted until near one o'clock. We at first took the best shelter we could find, but soon found that we must be wet and thought that we might as well be wet walking as standin(g); and so traveled on and came to the Lake just as the first shower was over, as wet as water could make us. We eat our Dinners & Just as we had done, a second shower came up with just as much wind as set the Lake in motion; the swell rose to about 3 ft high and foamed on the shore. We then prepared to survey the Road Back to Ja-tocque Lake and set off wet as we were and surveyed 2½ miles and took up our Quarters in an old Indian Cabbin.

THURSDAY, July 15th.—We started early as our clothes were still wet notwithstanding all the pains we could take. We had this day as much rain as was sufficient to keep the Bushes wet; we how-ever made all possible haste, and Got Back to our camp a half after 10 o'clock, verry wet and sufficiently tired. We found the Distance between the lakes to be Nine Miles and a Quarter, along the old Road, a nearer way might be found but perhaps the ground might be much worse. Lake Erie is a fresh water sea; from its shore you can see the Horision and water meet.

FRIDAY, July 16th.—Set out after Breakfast on our return, and had the Lake in fine order, the wind and waves subsiding. We made all the Speed we could and reached the out Let of the Lake about the middle of the afternoon. We continued to push towards our camping place on the Alegina until night.

SATURDAY, July 17th.—Set off early and continued to make the Best way with our canoe, all hands working and Reached the camp where we had left Gibbons just before Dark. From the mouth of Cannowango to Lake Erie, we compute it to be Eighty miles to go by water; the greater part of this Distance is through a verry Rich Soil. From the head of the Jatocque Lake along the old French Road is nine miles & a Quarter.

SUNDAY, July 18th.—Passed Down the Creek. In the morning met Mr Adlum and his party; he had returned from his Trip the Evening before, and was then making a survey. We passed on and agreed to wait for him at the lower end of an Indian Town called Brokenstraw,* which had been distroyed in the last war by General Broadhead. Before we had quite reached the place of our destination we were obliged to put on shore. A verrey heavy rain was comming on, we had just time to Pitch our markee before the heavy rain came, and as our markee was Pitched and not much short of the Place where we were to wait for Adlum we concluded to wait there.

MONDAY, July 19th.—We proceeded down the Alegina; the river had a considerable fall, and the men worked hard, we went as we computed at the Rate of 4 miles & one half in the hour. We kept close to our canoe all day and came something better than thirty miles.

---

* The Brokenstraw Creek enters the Allegheny River about five miles below the town of Warren. An Indian town called Buckaloon, or Brokenstraw, once stood near the mouth of the creek, which was destroyed by a detachment under Colonel Broadhead, from Pittsburg, in 1781. It required a siege of some days to drive out the Indians, who retreated to the high hills in the rear of the village. Colonel Daniel Broadhead is supposed to have been born at Albany about 1725. His father migrated to Pennsylvania in 1738 and settled at a place he called (after his own name) Dansbury, now East Stroudsburg, in Monroe County. Young Broadhead endured many privations during the Indian wars. In 1771 he settled in Reading and was soon afterwards appointed Deputy Surveyor under John Lukens. In 1776 he was appointed Lieutenant Colonel of the Rifle Regiment and bore a conspicuous part in the Revolution. In the reorganization of the army in 1781 he was made Colonel of the First Regiment, and subsequently rose to the rank of a Brigadier. He afterwards served in the General Assembly, and in 1789 was appointed Surveyor General of the State, and held the office for eleven years. General Broadhead died at Milford, Pike County, November 15, 1809.—*See Pennsylvania Archives, New Series, Vol. X., p.* 645.

TUESDAY, July 20th.—We continued our Route Down the River and arrived at Fort Frankland* about 4 o'clock, and were kindly Recd by the commanding officer, Lieut. Jeffres, who seemed to be Desirous of oblidging us. On our way, about 4 miles above French (Creek), I killed a Catfish that weighed 10½ ℔ with Mr Adlum's Jacob Staff. We this day came by our Computation 20 miles; the whole distance from the mouth of Cannowango to French creek, supposed to be about 60 miles.

WEDNESDAY, July 21st.—Breakfasted with the commanding officer in the Garrison, and as we were out of Bread, and as several of the men had their feet sore with scalding, we concluded to stay at the fort this day and Get some Bread Baked, and let the men Rest one day. We dined and supped with the commanding officer who was exceedingly obliging and attentive.

THURSDAY, July 22d.—We this morning paid off and discharged an old Indian Cheiff and a white Shavage, which we had taken into pay at the Valley in the mountain, and are preparing to start for Lebueff.† Left the Fort at 2 o'clock in company with the other commissioners, mounted and equiped in such a manner as Beggars all Description; the appointments of the Vicar of Wake-

---

*Fort Franklin was located near the mouth of French Creek. Old Fort Venango, as it was called by the English, was erected here in 1754 by the French. It was called by them Fort Machault, after a celebrated French financier and politician. When the French abandoned the place in 1759 they blew up the fort and burned their stores. Fort Franklin was built in 1787 by a detachment of 87 United States troops, from Pittsburg, under the command of Captain Hart. A garrison of 100 men was kept there until 1796. The town of Franklin, which was laid out by General William Irvine and Andrew Ellicott, under the act of 1795, is now a thrifty and pretty little city of nearly 6,000 inhabitants.

†Fort LeBoeuf was located at what is now Waterford, on French Creek, in Erie County. In the early French Archives the stream was called Riviere aux Bœufs; in the Pennsylvania Archives it is simply translated into English as the "Beef River," or the "Buffalo River," because buffaloes were found there by the early explorers. It was also called the Venango by the English, a name corrupted from the Seneca term, In-un-gah, from which the word Weningo, and later Venango, doubtless sprang. The present name, French Creek, appears to have been given the stream by George Washington during his visit to the French there in 1753, by direction of Governor Dinwiddie, of Virginia.

field's family Going to Church would not bear comparrison. Our intention was to go to Mr Mead's at Cassouaggo that night; as we had previously started our Canoes and all hands, with orders to make the best of their way to that place. We rode on at the utmost speed our cattle could make, in the manner they and us were appointed, untill after dark, hoping every moment to come to some house, when to our Great disapointment we Lost the path, and had no resorce but to take up our Quarters and go to sleep. Before morning a heavy rain came on; we had no camp and were obliged to take it as it came. When the morning came our horses were gone and we were obliged not only to take up our Beds, but our horse Furniture, and walk. We found it five miles to Mr Mead's.

FRIDAY, July 23d.—Came to Mr Meads, Got our Breakfast and took a walk to see Mr Mead's plantation* and Improvements. The

---

*David Mead was the first settler where the town of Meadville now stands. He was a native of Hudson, N. Y. His father, Darius Mead, when his son became of age, removed to Wyoming, where they both had purchased lands under the Pennsylvania title. Owing to the Connecticut troubles they abandoned their lands and settled near Northumberland. David Mead afterwards became a citizen of Sunbury, where he kept an inn for several years. After various discouraging struggles with fortune and the Indians, he left Sunbury to seek a home west of the Allegheny River. In 1788 he visited this section of the country, then a wilderness, with his brother John and several others. In 1789 he moved his family out. After years of toil and privation his prospects began to brighten, when another Indian war was threatened. Many fled, but Mr. Mead, having important interests at stake, remained. The Indian troubles were happily terminated by General Wayne in 1795. For several months in 1791, when the Indians were daily expected to attempt the extermination of the settlers on French Creek, Mr. Mead, with his family, resided at Franklin, so that they might be able to seek refuge in the fort in case of danger. During this time his father, who had followed him to his western home, was taken by two Indians from a field, where he was at work, and carried to the vicinity of Conneaut Lake, where he was afterwards found dead. One of his captors also laid dead near him, showing that there had been a severe struggle. In 1799 Mr. Mead became one of the associate judges for Crawford County. He was also a Major General in the militia. In size he stood six feet three, and was large in proportion. Of a vigorous mind, he was always actively engaged upon public or private business. His first wife was Agnes Wilson, of Northumberland County; his second, Janet Finney, daughter of Robert Finney, Esq. The Mead mansion was noted for the hospitality of its occupants. He died August 23, 1816, in the 65th year of his age.—*Alden's Magazine, Meadville*, 1816.

soil all along this creek Remarkably Rich; the Low Ground in particular in appearance the Richest I ever saw. We had sent off our men with the canoe and Baggage before us from Fort Frankland, and were in expectation that they would have joined this evening but are Disapointed.

SATURDAY, July 24th.—The men and canoe arrived. We immediately set of; Col'l Matlack and myself with four hands in the canoe & Mr Adlum with Neal St Clair and John Ria* whom we had taken into pay at Cassawaggo, by land; and appointed to met at Leboueff. We made the best way we could but were much interrupted with the Ripples and Sholes. About 1 o'clock we were stopped with a shower of rain; we made by our calculation about 8 miles this day and encamped.

SUNDAY, July 25th.—Set of(f) and made way as fast as Possable but were much Delayed and the men much fatigued by the Shoales and Ripples, where the men were obliged to Drag the canoe. By 12 o'clock we had got 10 miles as we computed when we stopped to Dine. I had felt for the two preceeding day(s) a soreness cross my kidneys, and while at Dinner I was stooping for a bit of meat I was taken with so sharp a pain that I had almost fallen. After Dinner was over we all got on Board; I laid on my Belley as the easiest position the crowded situation of the canoe would afford. After some time I wished to change my Position but was unable and was oblidged to Remain so untill the canoe stopped at night to encamp. After the tent was pitched and the fire kindled, the men assisted me, and with difficulty I got to the fire.

MONDAY, July 26th.—Unable to assist myself any way, can only move my hands and arms. The men put me on board the Canoe and proceeded up the creek. At 12 o'clock we arrived at the mouth of the Leboeuff Branch and found the water in (it) so low, that the men were oblidged to open a channel with the paddles to get fairly into the Branch. We proceeded only a little way further

---

* Properly, Rea.

until we met with another bar where the men were obliged to open a passage with the paddles. As Mr Adlum had arrived at the mouth of the Branch at 3 o'clock this morning and left a note informing us that we would find him encamped at the old Fort, about 3 miles above the mouth of the Branch, Colonel Matlack and Mathew Gray who was sick went on shore and took the Indian path; I was obliged to stay in the canoe being unable either to Rise or stand.

The men made all the way they could but were obstructed to such a degree by Shoale water and Driftwood, that when it was time to encamp we were not more than a mile from the mouth of the Branch. I Directed them to go on shore and encamp. As soon as they had got a fire made they carried me to it, and made a seat on which with difficulty I sat for some time. I then sent off Hicks to the uper camp to inform them that the canoe could not come up that night. He was on the way met by Neal St Clair and Jno Ria and returned. By St Clair & Ria I sent them some provision to their camp, as they were out. After sitting a while and taking some chocolate I felt something Better.

Tuesday, July 27th.—John Ria and Neal St Clair came from the uper camp and brought me a line from Colonel Matlack informing me what things and Provisions they wanted, and that they intended to start immediately for Lake Erie; I sent them the men provisions &c without any Delay, and here I am left unable to help myself, though much Better.

[Wednesday, Thursday, Friday and Saturday, the 28th, 29th, 30th and 31st, are blank.]

Sunday, August 1st.—We arrived at Fort Frankland about 3 o'clock. Though I continued to get something better, yet I mended but slowly. This afternoon I collected a small quantity of oyl* from a small oyl spring in the bank of French creek, with which I had my back rubbed before I went to bed.

---

*This was what was afterwards known as the famous Petroleum, or "Rock Oil." It was gathered by the Cornplanter Indians as it was found floating on the surface of the water. In after years the great oil field was developed in this region.

MONDAY, August 2d.—Felt something better and had my back rubbed with the oyl this morning. We spent the forenoon in preparing and fiting out a party to survey the Allegina River, but were prevented from sending them off by rain that came on about 12 o'clock.

TUESDAY, August 3d.—Started our surveying party and took the necessary measures to follow them as soon as possable. Set off about 3 o'clock Down the River but did not overtake the surveying party that day.

WEDNESDAY, August 4th.—Set off Down the River and about 9 o'clock passed the camp where the surveying party had slept the night Before, and overtook them in a short time afterwards. Left them and told them that we would encamp so as that they might come to us that night, which they Did accordingly.

THURSDAY, August 5th.—Started the Surveying party Early in the morning, as we were oblidged to Detain a while in order to Bake some Bread. As soon as that was done, we followed and overtook them, and gave them some provisions and then made the Best of our way for the mouth of Toby's Creek.* At 1 o'clock we had a heavy shower; after it was over we proceeded down the River, and came to the mouth of Toby's Creek about 5 o'clock, and Before we had time to pitch our tent we had another heavy shower followed by a Rainy night.

FRIDAY, August 6th.—The morning showery and continued so untill 12 o'clock, when it cleared up a little, but does not yet promise fair weather. Our Survey party not yet come, though it is now passed 4 o'clock. Surveying party came in before night, and after them John Rea and Fred'k Bawm† came to our Camp. It was therefore agreed that Bawm and Rea should be taken in to pay

---

* Now called the Clarion River. It empties into the Allegheny a short distance from the town of Clarion. It was called "Stump Creek" at one time as well as "Toby's."

† Properly Baum.

for four days, and that I with one hand in addition should survey the River Down to the Kishcaminitas * while the other commissioners were employed in Exploring the Toby's Creek.

SATURDAY, August 7th.—Started with my party and surveyed nine miles and a half & took up our quarters.

SUNDAY, August 8th.—Continued our survey 11 miles further down the River.

MONDAY, August 9th.—The morning rains and seems to threaten a Rainy day; the day continued showery but I started and continued the survey of the River. At night we encamped a little below the old Kittaning† town.

TUESDAY, August 10th.—Was obliged to spend the morning in baking. We camped the night Before a little way above the mouth of Crooked Creek, and in the lower end of the Kittaning Bottom. We continued our survey but were prevented from Reaching the Kishcaminitas by John Rea finding a part of the carrage of a cannon‡ which he striped of all its Iron; this he found near a small Island above the Kittaning. We encamped half a mile above the Junction of the Kishcaminitas with the Alegina River, and had I known we were so near, I would have come all the way.

[NOTE.—In the original the above entry is lined out, and for some unaccountable reason its substance is repeated in the following, thus leaving a hiatus of one day.]

WEDNESDAY, August 11th.—We were obliged to bake this morning which lost us some time, and after Dinner we lost 3 hours by John Rea, who found part of the carrage of a field piece and delayed us untill he took off the Irons, which prevented me from

---

* The Kishkiminetas River forms the southern boundary of Armstrong County, and empties into the Allegheny one mile north of Freeport. According to Heckewelder the name is corrupted from *Gieschgumanito*, signifying, make daylight.

† This was an Indian town of some importance at an early date. It was destroyed by Colonel John Armstrong, September 8, 1756. It was known among the Indians as Attigue.

‡ Probably abandoned during Armstrong's expedition, or by some other military party—possibly the French.

reaching the Kishcaminitas. We came within 200 rods of it, but did not Expect we were so near.

THURSDAY, August 12th.—Came to the junction of the Kishcaminitas with the Ohio river and finished my survey; found it to be 85¼ miles from the mouth of French Creek to the Kishcaminitas. Discharged John Rea and Frederick Bawm; they Proceeded on their way to Pitsburgh and Neal St Clair and I took up our camp on the west side of the Ohio opposite the Kishcaminitas. This day sold John Rea 16 lb Gun Powder, for which he is to send me 8 lb Best Beaver furr.

FRIDAY, SATURDAY AND SUNDAY, August 13th, 14th and 15th.— Waited for Mr Adlum and Colonel Matlack. Did nothing; only Removed my camp about a mile up the Kishcaminitas to the mouth of a small run on the south side of the creek.

MONDAY, August 16th.—Yet no account from Adlum and Matlack. The day showry with thunder.

TUESDAY, August 17th.—The morning Lowers a rains a Little, which together with my indisposition keeps me close to my tent. Yet no account from the Commissioners.

WEDNESDAY, August 18th.—Waited untill I'm intirely out of patience and yet not one word from the Commissioners; one whole week now spent but it is in vain to freet. Yesterday, several showers and last night a heavy rain, and it still keeps cloudy and rains a little. After dinner took a walk Down to the mouth of the River, and Saw our people comming down in their canoes. Mr Adlum and Colonel Matlack came on shoar to me at the mouth of the River and we walked up the Beach for my camp, but were overtaken with a middlin heavy shower on our way. We Got to the Camp and agreed to Remain there for that night.

THURSDAY, August 19th.—Got Ready Early in the morning and started up the Kishcaminitas River. Saw two white men on the River in a canoe. Continued to make all the speed we could untill

night and then took up our camp on the west side, or rather southwest side of River at the foot of a Rocky hill near the mouth of a
small spring.

FRIDAY, August 20th.—Continued our Jorney up the River and
arrived at the mouth of Loyalhannon* at one oclock; and as we
had had several days of showery weather and continued moistness
in the air, our Cloathes of every kind were Damp and Disagreeable,
and as the afternoon was a fine one we agreed to let the men rest
and Dry their Cloathes, and ours.   We had this day been attempting to procure some fresh Provisions on our way up, from the Inhabitants along the River, and had been unsucksesful; we therefore
sent off two of our men in order to procure either Butter or meat
of any kind.   They Returned with(out) Sucksess.

SATURDAY, August 21st.—As all our attempts yesterday to procure provisions had been fruitless, we were obliged to stay this day
in order to get a supply of Both flour and meat; we were Luckay
enough this morning to get the half of a Veal from one Samuel
Hoy, who lives a little way below the mouth of Loyalhanning,† and
sent off a man and horse to Denison's mill which is eight miles up
Loyalhanning creek, in order to procure some flour; the man is not
yet returned.

A little after Dark the man sent to mill returned and brought us
a small supply of flour and a few pounds of Butter.   We have to
acknowledge our obligations to Col'o Will'm Perrey, who furnished
us with a horse and sent his son to mill for us for the flour.   He
lives just above the mouth of Loyalhanning.

SUNDAY, August 22d.—The morning cloudy but so much time
already Elapsed we must make every possable Exertion to get
through our Bussness; we proceeded up the River about 10 miles
and encamped for the day.

---

*The Loyalhanna Creek runs northwestward through Westmoreland County,
and unites with the Conemaugh River at Saltsburg, to form the Kishkiminetas.

† Opposite the site of the present town of Saltsburg, Indiana County.

MONDAY, August 23d.—Proceeded up the River; met with great difficulty; on account of the Low water were obliged to drag our canoes over the Ripples and were able to get only about 8 miles. This day Encamped above an old Indian field on the southwest of the River; this field is Remarkable for the Great number of Bones we found in it.

TUESDAY, August 24th.—Pursued our Jorney up the River, and with all the Exerscions we could make it was 1 oclock before we had Got 3½ miles, & the men were quite Exausted with the Labour of Dragging the Canoes up the Ripples. We came on shore to Dine and before we had done, a rain came on which induced us to pitch our tents for the night. We employed the afternoon in trying to procure pack horses to carry our Baggage to Franks town and happily Succeeded.

WEDNESDAY, August 25th.—This morning we were Busseyley employed in adjusting the Loads for the horses. As soon as this was done we took our packs on our Backs, and started at 11 oclock and made the Best of our way up the River. We had got but a little way when we were overtaken by a smart shower at a place where we had no shelter of any kind. We proceeded up through the narrows where the River Cuts the Chesnut Ridge; these narrows are five miles in Length and the hill(s) come Down close to the water edge, so that we were obliged often to wade the River, and had Exceeding Bad walking as there was scarcely any Beech and the Rocks and Laurel come close to high water mark. We had Likewise several heavy shower(s) so that Between the wading the River and the Rain we were wet Indeed. About sunset we came to a house where one David Ingard lives, and took up our Quarters for the Night having Traveled about eight or nine miles.

THURSDAY, August 26th.—We set off early in the morning and proceeded up the River. Had much better walking this day and a fine clear day. We kept close to it, and arrived at the mouth of

Stony Creek* a little before sunset, and went up Stoney Creek half a mile to where one Daniel LaVere Lives, who Received us with an oppen Countenance. We this day came through the narrows formed by the Laurel Hill and found it in Gineral Good walking; we this day walked 19 or 20 miles.

By appointment our Pack horses were to meet us at the mouth of Stoney Creek, but we found they had been unable to Reach the place; we therfor took up our Quarters with Daniel LeVere for the night. As we were in a part of the country were none of us had ever Been we were obliged to hire a man and send off for one Clark to conduct us the nearest and best way from the Mouth of Stoney Creek to the mouth of Poplar run on the Frankstown Branch, through the Alegina mountain. We did in the evening after we had taken up our Quarters. As this messenger has to walk 18 miles to where Clark Lives, we can hardly Expect him to Return before the 28.

FRIDAY, August 27th.—Gersham Hicks came to us this morning and informed us that the horses and Baggage were comming; that they had been unable to Reach the fork Last night, the Road had been so Bad. After some time the horses came but on the way had Lost one of our Tents, for this tent two of our people were sent back who are not yet Returned. In the afternoon they Returned but could not find the tent altho they went back as far as the place they had Lodged the night Before; but they heard that a man and a Boy from the Jerseys had passed along the road between the time that our people returned to seek the tent, and as those people were in want of Cloathes as its said, no dout they played us a Jersey Trick.

---

*Bustling Johnstown, composed of an aggregation of eight municipalities stands here. When the Commissioners landed at the mouth of Stony Creek, ninety-seven years ago, in what was a dense wilderness, they doubtless never thought for a moment that in time immense iron works would be built in this wild canon, and that the roar and rattle of steam engines and passing railroad trains would awake the echoes of the mountain solitudes.

SATURDAY, August 28th.—We continued in our camp waiting the Return of young Levoy whom we had sent for Clark. He returned after sunset and with him a Daniel Clark, the man who had been Recomended was gon a hunting, and this man was the only person he could get to come who had any knowledge of the country through which we had to pass. This day we spent in Baking Bread and preparing for Crossing the Alegina, mendin Mokossins &c.

SUNDAY, August 29th.—Agreeable to the Resolution of the Last night we prepared this morning to survey the Conemaugh, as Mr D. Clark had refused to conduct us over the Mountains without we would Engage to pay him 10 shillings for every day that we would be from home. This we all agreed was unreasonable as he himself confessed that he was not fully acquainted with the country through which we must pass. We therefor paid for the day he had spent in comming and for another to go home in, 10 shillings, and prepared to go up through the narrows, and survey the creek, and sent our Baggage Round by a Better way with order to mett us Monday Night at the forks of Connemaugh; and as it was Expected they would be able to gain the forks much sooner than us, we set out first and proceeded up the creek as far as we could that day. Had bad walking and at night could scarcely find a spot to encamp on, for the Land which came to the waters edge for some miles together. We at length found a spot in the Laurel Large enough for us to lie on and took up our Quarters. Not long after Night rain came on and we were unprovided with any kind of shelter. This not only kept me uneasy for the moment but in pain in consequence as I was but verrey imperfectly Recovered from my former attack of the Rhumatisem, brought on in the same manner; and there I was in a country unsettled, without either canoe or horse.

MONDAY, August 30th.—Dryed my Cloathes with all the care I could, and took my Bundle on my Back, and so did my companions and we proceeded up the Creek with our survey and Gained the first forks of the Cr By ½ past 1 Oclock; there eat our Dinner and proceeded on untill night and encamped on the upper end of a Rock Bottom about two miles below the forks where the pack horses were to meet us. As we had given orders to the pack horse men in case that we Did not Reach the forks on Monday night that Hicks should be despatched down the Creek on Tuesday morning to meet us with Provisions, as we had taken only two Day(s) Provisions, we in order that they might know we were comming fired a Gun Twist after dark, but had no answer.

Tuesday, August 31st.—After Breakfast we went on with our survey and Reached the forks ½ after 10 oclock but found our people had not reached the place. We then enquired into the state of our provisions, and found that the whole we then had with us was not more than one scanty meal. We then judged it advisable to make the best speed we could to Frankstown and not wait Longer for the packhorses as we were certain either some mistake or misfortune had happened, or they would have been there before us. We accordingly set off at a N. E. course and surveyed 8 miles before Dark, but to our surprise we had not yet reached the State Road. The evening was Cloudy and we encamped by the side of a Laurel Thicket near a Small Branch of the Connemaugh.

Wednesday, September 1st.—The evening before we had divided our Provisions into Equal Shares, and though we had walked the whole day, yet each man's portion when he had it was so small; and not knowing how far we must travel before we could meet with any supply, none of us ventured to eat any supper. This morning every man cooked his own Chocolate with the utmost care and attention, and in General eat with the Chocolate about one-half of our Bread; and so we set out and in about 1½ hours we came to the State Road * about Eight miles N. W. of Blair's mill.

---

* On the 29th of March, 1787, an act of Assembly was passed appointing commissioners "to lay out a State highway, between the waters of the Frankstown branch of the Juniata and the river Conemaugh." This road, which is the one

After Traveling about 4 miles on this Road we eat the Remainder of our Provisions and Reached Mr Blair's mill a Little after 12 oclock where we were Rece'd with Great kindness by Mr Blair's family, who gave us our dinner, as neither Mr Blair* nor his wife were at home.   In the Evening Mrs Blair came home; and to my surprise Soon informed me that she knew something of me and my connections.   Upon enquring she is the daughter of a Mr Sims who was a friend and aquaintance of Mr R Plunketts† in Ireland, and came to this country the same year that Mr. Plunket came to the country; and is a verrey Decent, well Breed woman, and was very oblidging and attentive to us.   In the Evening we sent one of our men over to Patrick Cassidy's with a Note, Requesting him to come to us in the morning.

referred to by Mr. Maclay, is still known as the Frankstown road. It crossed the Allegheny Mountains and reached the Conemaugh at Johnstown. April 10, 1792, the Conemaugh and its branches were declared public highways by act of the Legislature.

*John Blair, Jr., was one of the early settlers in the territory embraced in Blair County, and after him the county was named. His home was some four miles west of Hollidaysburg, on the Huntingdon, Cambria and Indiana turnpike, formerly known as the "Northern Pike." He was in his day a man of mark and foremost in every public enterprise.—*A. K. Bell, D. D., in Egle's Hist. Pa., p.* 397.

† It is proper in this connection to clear up the history of the Plunkets. William Plunket, the first presiding justice of Northumberland County, died in the spring of 1791, at Sunbury, aged about 100 years. He was the father of Mrs. Samuel Maclay, whose lineage is traceable to John Harris, Sr., whose grave is yet to be seen on the bank of the river at Harrisburg, in front of the residence of Gen. Simon Cameron. John Harris, Sr., died in 1748. His wife, Esther Say, was a lady of rare endowments, who came from England, in the family of Judge Shippen. Among their children were John, the proprietor of Harrisburg; Samuel, who settled at the outlet of Cayuga Lake, New York, and a daughter, who married Dr. William Plunket. The latter, at the time of his marriage, resided at Carlisle, and his daughters, four in number, were born there. His wife dying early, he remained a widower, which fact gave rise to the mistake of some authors in stating that he was a bachelor. His daughters were Elizabeth, born in 1755, married to Samuel Maclay, the writer of this journal; Isabella, born January, 1760, married to William Bell, Esq., of Elizabethtown, N. J.; Margaret, married to Isaac Richardson, removed to Wayne County, N. Y., then known as the Genesee Country. Hester Plunket, the youngest, married Col. Robert Baxter, of the British army, and died about a year after her marriage. Her daughter married Dr. Samuel Maclay, of Mifflin County. John Harris' wife, Elizabeth McClure,

THURSDAY, September 2d.—After Breakfast Mr Cassidy came and informed us that he was unacquainted with the Ground between this and Connemaugh further than the head of the Poplar Run, but he was of the opinion that the Poplar Run Gap was a much Better Gap than the one in which the Road is now made; and informed us that if we pleased he would Go with and Likewise procure some other person who knew the country all the way, to go with him and us in order to view the Poplar Gap, and the Ground beyond the head of the Poplar Run as far as the forks of Connemaugh. He likewise promised to assist us in getting horses to carrey our Baggage down as far as Water Street, and his assistance in Procuring us some fresh Provisions.

FRIDAY, September 3d.—After Breakfast we Rec'd a note from Mr Cassidy that he had the promise of two horses and two sheep for one of which we sent one of our people. Not until 4 oclock this day did we hear anything from our Pack horses. Then they came in. They had mistaken the forks of Conemaugh where they were to wait for us and stopped at the first, instead of going on to the second, and by that mistake have Lost us 2 days. Some time after night our man Returned with a Mutton.

---

said to have been the most lovely woman of her day, died young, from fright and grief, at the report of her husband's death, which however proved untrue. Her daughter, Mary Harris, who inherited much of her mother's beauty, married William Maclay, the first United States Senator from Pennsylvania, and brother of Samuel, the surveyor. The latter's wife, and Mrs. William Maclay, were cousins and they married brothers.

William C. Plunket, Lord Chancellor of Ireland, was a nephew of Doctor Plunket. A brother of Doctor Plunket came to this country, bringing with him a daughter, Margaret, who married Samuel Simmons, of Pine Creek, who resided a few miles west of Jersey Shore. His name was Robert, and he is the man alluded to by Mrs. Blair. The celebrated Dr. Plunket died at Sunbury in the office afterwards owned by Ebenezer Greenough. He was totally blind during the closing years of his life. His will is dated January 3, 1791, and proved May 25, 1791, in which he mentions his granddaughter, Margaret Baxter, one of the most beautiful and accomplished ladies of the State, who died at Milroy, Mifflin County, July 6, 1863. The three sisters, Mrs. Maclay, Mrs. Ball and Mrs. Richardson, survived to a good old age, and resided together in Mifflin County. For the facts in this condensed history of the Plunkets I am indebted to *Linn's Annals of Buffalo Valley, pages* 271—2.

SATURDAY, September 4th.—This morning we sent off a part of our Baggage to Mr Cassidy's by a son of McCunes who brought us the mutton. Mr Adlum was this morning Imployed in protracting our works from the mouth of Stoney creek. After Breakfast and after I had finished coppying my note(s) I took 2 hands, and Began at the 50 mile Tree above Mr Blairs and surveyed the Road to Patrick Cassidys, and from thence to the mouth of Poplar Run, which Bussness was some time Delayed By the Rain, which fell this Day. Mr Adlum finished his work and Joined us in the afternoon. We Likewise Got a horse from Mr Cassidy and Got another Load of our Baggage brought over this day from our camp at Mr Blair's, but Gersham Hicks with the Remainder was still Behind at the Camp.

SUNDAY, September 5th.—We Despatched Seymor with a horse this morning to Mr Blair's to bring forward Hicks and the Remainder of our Baggage; and took the necessary measures in order to Explore the Ground up through the Poplar Gap, and thence to the forks of Connemaugh. The man we sent is not yet Returned. In the mean time we had verrey differant accounts of the Ground through the Poplar Gap. Patrick Cassidy told us that he had been at the head of the Poplar run and five miles further towards the forks of Connemaugh; that so far it was Excelent Ground for a Road; much Better than the road through the other Gap, and insinuated that undue means had been exercised or the State Road would have been taken through the Poplar Gap. This Representation was Coroborated by one William Pringle who undertook to show us an Exceeding Good way for a road up through the Poplar Gap. To this a young man, a hunter, of the name of Shirley, Replyd that he knew the Poplar Gap well; that he had had a hunting camp on it near the head; that there was no place there that would admit of a Road; that if Pringle could find a Road there, then he Shirley would Give them his head for a foot ball. But he informed us that there might be a Road had to Connemaugh by

Beginning at the East end of a Ridge that is south of the Poplar run and keeping that Ridge up to the Blue Knob a mountain so called in those parts, and from thence by keeping the dividing Ridge, but this way was objected to by Cassidy and others as Going quite too far out of the way. Shirley further informed us that Pringle, who was to be our Gide had some time before undertaken to conduct a Company over to Connemaugh & had Lost himself and with Difficulty found the way home. From all these circumstances, and acct taken together we were Determined to see the Ground and set out with our party and surveyed about 2¼ miles up the Poplar run through Low swampy Ground Inclined to be stoney.

MONDAY, September 6th.—Continued our survey up the poplar run through stoney swampy Bottoms, much cut into Gulleys by the water for about 2 miles; then took over a hill and struck the run again. Found the Ground much the same up to the second forks, where Pringle told us we must take the mountain which we did and found it much too steep to answer for a road. However we continued our survey untill we came in sight of a cove in the hill, I then in order to save time proposed to Leave the compass and walk up to the top of the hill in order to obtain a view of the hills around us as by this time I had abundant Testimony that we could place no Dependance upon the Information of our Gides. When we had Reached the top of the first Rise or Spur of the mountain I planely saw that admitting the Ground to have been good to the Bottom of the hill there was no Possability of making a Road and therefore under these circumstances Gave it as my opinion that to prosecute the Bussness farther would be misspending our time and wasting the Publick Money; Cassidy still Persisted that there could be a fine Road made there, and Colonel Matlack said he had wished to have Discussed this matter among ourselves, as Commissioners and not before any other persons, and concluded with Expressing a Desire of seeing the top of the hill but added that he would not bear an imputation of wasting the publick money. I

Replyd that for my own part I had seen sufficient to fix my opinion; if he or any other person had not, that an hour or two would be Sufficient for the purpose, that under these considerations I had no objections to going on to the top of the hill.

Mr Adlum Lickewise thought it best to Proceed with the survey to the top of the hill; and we proceeded accordingly but before we had gone a half a mile further we plainly saw that our Gides were utterly at a Loss, and in a short time Cassidy himself Declared that there could not be a road made there, and Longe Before we had Reached the Top of the mountain, we were all willing to return back the best way we could find through the Laurel. We got down a little below the forks of the run and took up our Quarters, heartily tired of Road hunting. Cassidy and Pringle would not stay with (us) all night, though they were invited.

Tuesday, September 7th.—We returned to Cassidys and got there a little before 11 oclock. Were oblidged to wait some time in order to procure horses to bring forward our Baggage and had to send one of our people to Mr Blair's mill to get a fresh supply of flour. This Detained Mr Adlum all night at Cassidys. After Dinner I took two men to Carrey Chain, and began the survey of the Frankstown Branch at the mouth of Poplar run, and Proceed Down as far as Franks old town,* When night came on, and not meeting with any of our people, Colonel Matlack and I went to Lowery's and staid all night. When I Left off surveying I had sent the chain carriers up to one Tituses to see whether any of our

---

* Frankstown, Blair County, is probably the oldest place on the Juniata River, traders having mentioned it as early as 1750. The Indian town was located at the mouth of a small run, and at one time contained a considerable number of inhabitants. The Indian name was *Assunepachla*, which signifies a meeting of the waters, as several streams unite here and form the Juniata. The Indians abandoned it in 1755. The name Frankstown comes from an old German Indian trader named Stephen Franks, who lived contemporaneously with old Hart, after whom Hartslog Valley was named. Franks was a great friend of the Indians and lived and died among them, and it was after his death that one of the chiefs took his name, which caused the erroneous impression that the name was given to the town in honor of the chief.—*Jones' Juniata Valley, pages* 324-5.

people had come there.   On their way they met with N. St Clair
who Mr Adlum had sent with our Blankets and part of the Baggage; but the night was so dark that they could not find the road
to Lowerys.   They therefore took up camp on the Branch.

WEDNESDAY, September 8th.—Left Lowery's after Breakfast, and
came to the camp that the men had made on the Branch; where
Mr Adlum had Got Before us.   We were still at a Loss for the
means of conveying our Baggage.   Mr Adlum had hired Cassidy's
Boy to bring our Baggage to Frankstown, and he agreed to take it
a little further.   We then proceeded with the survey; Cassidy's
Boy carried our Baggage about two miles Down the Branch, where
he left us to shift.   We then prevailed on a Duchman to Lend us
a Canoe; into which we packed our things and proceeded about 1½
miles further, and encamped.   Colonel Matlack Bough(t) some
motton from a Duchman to be Delivered in the morning, and was
Lickwise in Treaty with the same man for a canoe.

THURSDAY, September 9th.—Rec'd the motton and Bought a
canoe provided we Licke it when we see it; and are preparing to
set out again.   Set of(f) and came to where the canoe was.   We
were obliged to take it altho it was as ugly a one as possable.   We
got our Baggage on Board and Proceeded down the River;* we
found the water so low that the men were obliged to Drag nearly
one half of the Distance which Delayed us Exceedingly.   We went
on and pitched upon a camp and Kindled a fire, but the men were
so Exausted with the Extream Fatigue that it was past Eight
oclock before the could reach the place, altho we had come only
about 3 miles.

FRIDAY, September 10th.—We continued our survey down the
River & made about 6 miles this Day; the water Low, and the
Banks of the River Rocky and Bushey.

SATURDAY, September 11th.—Continued the survey of the River
and with all the Exercesions we could make we only got seven

----
* The Little Juniata.

miles with our survey.   The walking on the river bad & the water too Low.

SUNDAY, September 12th.—Proceeded down the River with our survey.   Colonel Matlack and myself walked along the shore with the surveyor(s) untill we got below the place called the Fiddle Strings.   We then concluded, as there was no obstruction in the River from there to Water Street, that we would take the road, which we did accordingly and came to Water Street.*   Came down through the narrows to the house of one Brown, where we intended waiting for Mr Adlum, and the canoe; but after some time we were informed by Brown that Coll'o Cannon was to start the next morning for Phila'd.   We concluded to leave a note for Mr Adlum with Brown and go on to Coll Cannon's.   We did so; came to Coll Cannon's; found that he was at meeting.   However we found means to procure a dinner.   After some time the family came home, and Expresed their Satisfaction at seeing us & treated us with kindness.   We then learned that the Col'o had a Brother Lately arrived from Ireland, whose family was then near W(il)-mington; that he was going down with a Horse to assist them in coming up.   Coll. Matlack determined to take this oppertunity to get on his way as far as Lancaster.   Night came on and not ac-count from Mr Adlum and our canoe party.

MONDAY, September 13th.—Early in the Morning Mr Adlum came to us at Col'l Cannon's.   He had compleated the survey yes-terday at 3 oclock and came down part of the way with the canoe, but stopt to speak with a man on the road near a Bent in the River; then went on to the next Bent where the water appeared in good order for canoeing, & after Looking up and Down, and not

---

* Two miles above Alexandria, Huntingdon County. Water Street is an old place and was settled prior to the Revolution. A stream of water from Canoe Mountain, supposed to be the Arch Spring, of Sinking Valley, passes down a ravine and empties into the Juniata at this place. For some distance through a narrow defile the road passed directly through the bed of this stream, a circum-stance which induced the settlers to call it Water Street.—*Jones' Juniata Valley*, *page* 301.

seeing the canoe, concluded that they were ahead and went on to one Mitchells where they were to stop. When he came there they were not come nor did they come that night. He therefore Dispatched Hicks, this morning to Look for them. After Breakfast we all walked down to the river, and found they were just arrived. We then concluded as it was so Difficult to proceed with the canoe to leave her and all our Baggage, our Coats and Papers Excepted, and make the best of our way home. Col'l Matlack was Provided with a horse; and Mr Adlum and myself Determined to take part of our Baggage on our Backs and foot it home. We got all our Baggage on shore and got the things that were to be left carried up to Coll Cannon's. We packed the other things up in order, took our Back Loads and set out. Col'l Cannon was so obludging as to accomodate us with a horse as far as Huntingdon, where we arrived at 3 oclock. We spent some time with Col'l Matlack in arranging our bussness and set off for Kishacoquillis at——* oclock with our Baggage on our Backs; we had one half of the City to admire us, ——* they looked at us with attention. We walked 4 miles came to one Silles and took up our Quarters for the night; attempted to procure a man and horse to carry our Baggage (and have?) hopes of Success.

TUESDAY, September 14th.—Though we had hopes last night of procuring a packhorse, yet when the morning came, the man would not go; we therefor took up our loads and set off; traveled 6 miles to the Improvement of a Duchman, who for half a dollar agreed to carry our things into Kishicoquillis valley. Agreed with him, put the Baggage into a horse Load, fixed it on and made the best of our way. Came into the valley to James Logan's† who with one

---

*Torn off.

† This beautiful valley was named after Kishicoquillas, an old Indian chief who had his cabin there at an early day. Logan, the celebrated Mingo chief, afterwards dwelt in the valley. But the Logan alluded to by Mr. Maclay could hardly be the famous son of Shikellamy. Mr. Maclay did much surveying in the valley, and afterwards some of his descendants lived and died there.

——* horses carried our things to John Wilson, who carried them to Robert McLain; where we all arrived a little after.

WEDNESDAY, September 15th.—Agreed with Robert McLain for a horse and boy pr Day to carry us to Buffaloe and set off in the ——* Mr Adlum and myself stopped this day at Mr ——*, and sent the men with the horse forward.

THURSDAY, September 16th.—Set out from ——* in the morning and about 4 oclock overtook ——* with the Baggage. Traveled about 3 miles further to ——* newcombers in Mussers Valley and put up for the night.

FRIDAY, September 17th.—Set off in the morning; walked very (constantly?) untill one oclock, when I reached home. Found my family all well and at Dinner. Our men came about 2 hours afterwards.

[On pages 11–12 a portion of the history of John Adlum is given in a foot note. Since those pages were printed information as to the dates of his birth and death has been received. John Adlum was the son of Joseph and Catharine Adlum, and he was born in York, Pa., April 29, 1759. At the age of 54 he married his cousin, Miss Margaret Adlum, daughter of John Adlum, of Frederick, Md. They had two children, Margaret C., now Mrs. Barber, of Georgetown, D. C., and Anna Maria, afterwards Mrs. H. H. Dent. They lived for several years near Havre de Grace, when Mr. Adlum moved to Montgomery County, Md., where he lived for a few years. His last change of residence was to "The Vineyard," two miles from Georgetown, where he died March 1, 1836, in the 77th year of his age. He was a soldier in the Revolution, a Major in the Provisional Army during the administration of the elder Adams, and afterwards a Brigadier General in the militia of Pennsylvania. As a scientific agriculturist he had few superiors. He devoted almost the whole of his life to the acquisition and diffusion of useful information. In early life he was acquainted with Dr. Joseph Priestly, of Northumberland, and the knowledge of chemical science, which he learned from that eminent philosopher, he applied with signal success to various agricultural operations. His wife died at the residence of his son-in-law, Mr. C. Barber, in Georgetown, July 16, 1852, at the age of 86. His eldest daughter, Mrs. Barber, is the only one of the family now alive. She has one son, living in Maryland. Anna Maria, the youngest daughter, had four children, most all of whom are living in Pennsylvania. Miss Mary Huckell, of Muncy, Pa., (now 80 years old,) remembers seeing John Adlum when a child. She describes him as being a tall, stout, muscular man, and active in his movements. He had blue eyes, light hair,

———
* Torn off.

a florid complexion and a face smooth shaven.   His manners were lively and jovial.   She says that he was exceedingly well informed on all subjects and was a great talker.   His disposition was mild and equitable.   He was very benevolent and loved to aid the needy and unfortunate.]

REPORTS ON THE SURVEY.

In 1789 the "Society for Promoting the Improvement of Road and Inland Navigation" was formed, and had in a short time one hundred members residing in various parts of the State. Surveys of the Schuylkill, Susquehanna, Juniata and other streams were authorized, with the view of ascertaining the cost of the proposed water ways to connect with the lakes, to bring the trade to Philadelphia. In 1791 the Society, through Robert Morris, submitted a report and memorial to the Legislature, giving a comprehensive view of the various routes for canals and roads, with estimates of the expense. It may be curious to compare their ideas and views, and estimates, with those entertained at the present day, so far as the same routes have been pursued. Extracts from the report of Maclay, Adlum and Matlack are given herewith:

Susquehanna navigation, as connected with the Schuylkill on the east, and Ohio and the great lakes on the west. From Philadelphia to Pittsburg:

	Miles.	Chs.
Up Schuylkill to the mouth of the Tulpehocken	61	00
Up Tulpehocken to the end of the proposed canal	37	09
Length of the canal	4	15
Down Quitapahilla to Swatara	15	20
Down Swatara to Susquehanna	23	00
Up Susquehanna to Juniata	23	28
Up Juniata to Huntingdon	86	12
From Huntingdon, on Juniata, to mouth of Poplar Run	42	00
Portage to the Canoe Place on Conemaugh	18	00
Down Conemaugh to Old Town at the mouth of Stoney Creek	18	00
Down Conemaugh and Kishkiminetas to Allegheny River	69	00
Down Allegheny River to Pittsburg on the Ohio	29	00
Total	425	84

ESTIMATE OF THE EXPENSE.

Schuylkill from the tide water to Reading, by David Rittenhouse and others...£	1,147 00
By Benjamin Rittenhouse and John Adlum....................................	1,519 13
Clearing the Tulpehocken by do..	1,419 90
The canal from Tulpehocken to Quitapahilla, 20 feet wide and 7 feet on an average.*..	
The Quitapahilla and Swatara..	18,900 00
Susquehanna from Swatara to Juniata..	300 00
The Juniata to Frank's Town...	2,320 00
Canal or lock navigation to Poplar Run (if found necessary, which will probably not be the case)..	7,000 00
Portage of 18 miles to Conemaugh at £20 per mile...........................	360 00
Conemaugh and Kishkiminetas to Allegheny..................................	7,150 00

In order to reach Presque Isle by the Juniata, Conemaugh, Allegheny and French Creek route the following estimate was submitted:

	Miles.	Chs.
To the mouth of Kishkiminetas, by the same route as above..................	397	04
Up the Allegheny to French Creek..	83	43
Up French Creek to Le Bœuf..	65	40
Portage from Le Bœuf to Presque Isle...	15	40
Total..	561	27

The sum of £500 for French Creek, and £400 for the Portage, is all the additional expense in the navigation from Kishkiminetas to Presque Isle or the lakes.

FROM PHILADELPHIA BY WEST BRANCH.

From Philadelphia to Presque Isle by the West Branch of the Susquehanna, Sinnemahoning and Conewango:

	Miles.	Chs.
From Philadelphia to Swatara as above...	140	44
Up Susquehanna to the West Branch, at Sunbury..............................	65	00
Up the West Branch to the mouth of Sinnemahoning..........................	106	00
Up Sinnemahoning to the Forks...	15	20
Up the North Branch of Sinnemahoning...	19	40
By the Portage to the head of Allegheny River..................................	23	00
Down Allegheny River (partly through New York State) to the mouth of Conewango..	76	00
Up Conewango to New York line 11 miles—thence up the same through the State of New York 17 miles to Chautauqua Lake........................	28	00
Across Chautauqua Lake to its head...	17	00
Portage to Lake Erie at the mouth of Chautauqua Creek.....................	9	20
Along Lake Erie to Presque Isle..	25	00
Total..	524	44

* Here the Society left a blank.

Another route to the lake is also given as follows:

	Miles.	Chs.
From Philadelphia to the Forks of Sinnemahoning, as before	326	64
Up the West Branch of Sinnemahoning	24	00
Portage to Little Toby's Creek	14	00
Down Little Toby's Creek to the main branch	10	00
Down the main branch of Little Toby's Creek to the Allegheny	70	00
Up the Allegheny to French Creek	35	00
Up French Creek and the Portage to Presque Isle	81	00
Total	560	64

No estimate of costs accompanies these routes.

Metalmark Books is a joint imprint of The Pennsylvania State University Press and the Office of Digital Scholarly Publishing at The Pennsylvania State University Libraries. The facsimile editions published under this imprint are reproductions of out-of-print, public domain works that hold a significant place in Pennsylvania's rich literary and cultural past. Metalmark editions are primarily reproduced from the University Libraries' extensive Pennsylvania collections and in cooperation with other state libraries. These volumes are available to the public for viewing online and can be ordered as print-on-demand paperbacks.

LIBRARY OF CONGRESS CATALOGING-IN-PUBLICATION DATA

Maclay, Samuel, 1741–1811.
Journal of Samuel Maclay while surveying the west Branch of the Susquehanna, the Sinnemahoning and the Allegheny rivers in 1790 / Samuel Maclay ; annotated by John F. Meginness.
p.   cm.
Summary: "A journal, originally published in 1887, describing a 1790 surveying expedition to explore newly purchased land in northwestern Pennsylvania. Includes historical annotations by John F. Meginness"—Provided by publisher.
ISBN 978-0-271-05647-0 (pbk. : alk. paper)
1. Maclay, Samuel, 1741–1811—Diaries.
2. Maclay, Samuel, 1741–1811—Travel—Pennsylvania.
3. Pennsylvania—Description and travel—Early works to 1800.
4. Susquehanna River—Description and travel—Early works to 1800.
5. Sinnemahoning Creek (Pa.)—Description and travel—Early works to 1800.
6. Allegheny River (Pa. and N.Y.)—Description and travel—Early works to 1800.
7. Frontier and pioneer life—Pennsylvania—Sources.
8. Explorers—Pennsylvania—Diaries.
9. Surveyors—Pennsylvania—Diaries.
I. Meginness, John Franklin, 1827–1899.
II. Title.
F153.M11 2012
917.48'5043—dc23
2012023583

Printed in the United States of America
Reprinted by The Pennsylvania State University Press, 2012
University Park, PA 16802-1003